Sense of Direction

By Marlene Koestenblatt Kushner, EdD

Auctus Publishers

www.auctuspublishers.com

To my dear friend Brian
With love & appreciation
Marlene

Book and Cover Design by Colleen J. Cummings

Published by Auctus Publishers
606 Merion Avenue, First Floor
Havertown, PA 19083
Printed in the United States of America

ISBN 979-8-9868429-7-4
Library of Congress Control Number: 2023947592

For Nick and Erik

* * *

Two roads diverged in a wood
and I took the one less traveled by
And that has made all the difference

The above lines are taken from one of the most studied poems in the English language. In reading analyses of the poem, two distinct themes emerge. One interpretation states that Robert Frost expressed the rewards of investing oneself in the uncharted, the unknown. The other is that he gave voice to the inevitable regret that an individual feels over opportunities lost due to the choices one has made. I believe the two interpretations are mutually compatible. Both capture how I view the long course of my life.

It has been profoundly satisfying to work with students who have managed to survive and thrive within therapeutic and educational systems. These students persevere, grateful for resources offered, determined to realize a better life for themselves and their family members. It takes great strength and motivation to persist, given the challenges they have encountered and overcome. I am indeed privileged to support these students who are both inspired and inspiring. I dedicate this book to them and to the invested and compassionate individuals who have supported and encouraged me to "pass it on." My mother was the first of many to do so.

Preface

What comes into your mind when you hear the word "invisible?" In a symbolic sense, this quality can be an advantage. For example, invisibility would be a valuable quality for a sleuth or for someone who is seeking to pass, unidentified. Conversely, it can be a disadvantage, when one feels unworthy of notice, of attention. Have you had the experience of "being invisible?" What was the experience like? I imagine that each of us has, at some time, wished that we were invisible. In all likelihood, most of us would also have appreciated being set apart from the proverbial crowd, being extolled for our uniqueness, our contributions. You may be wondering what I am writing about: What is my point? Readers, I am prompting you to think about how you see, how you understand yourself, and how you believe you are seen by others. For many of us with "invisible disabilities," our self-understanding is limited, as well as misunderstood. Those who interact or have relationships with us may be puzzled, frustrated, or disbelieving when they observe behaviors or hear our self-definitions, which are inconsistent with the view they have of us. What are "invisible disabilities?" They are disorders that generally become apparent via their behavioral manifestations rather than due to the disabling conditions themselves. In contrast to sensory or motor disabilities, such as blindness or paralysis, they become evident when the situation requires a vulnerable or deficit function that cannot be compensated for and for which there is not sufficient support. An example would be a severely dyslexic student who does not have access to either an audio version of material or a reader. Any disability, invisible or apparent, can be a challenge or obstacle, depending on the circumstances. However, having an "invisible disability" presents both advantages and disadvantages. It is possible to "pass," sometimes indefinitely, or until compensation is no longer possible. "Passing" can be very costly in terms of the consequences. However, choosing to reveal a disability also poses risks. I will go into detail about these options later in the book. While there are many medical conditions that are invisible, I focus on those of which I have experience, or which I have assisted students in overcoming.

Once I was diagnosed as having learning disabilities, I dedicated myself to understanding learning differences/disorders and the often profound impact they have upon our lives and on those who love and work with us. Having suffered multiple misdiagnoses, I was determined to obtain a doctorate in neuropsychology, specializing in learning disorders.

Unfortunately, I have found that there is limited information and outright misinformation about "invisible disabilities" among the general public. Furthermore, not enough practitioners in healthcare and education have the requisite training to serve this complex and heterogeneous population. Finally, I have been frustrated and saddened to learn that this is also true for too many in my profession. This ignorance often fuels poor treatment outcomes as well as discrimination. Suffering from the socio-cultural barriers and economic losses resulting from the above realities opened my mind and heart to the need for this book. Nevertheless, I was conflicted. Much of my life had been an attempt to protect myself from the painful consequences of revealing my vulnerabilities. Ultimately, my commitment to empower students to understand, accept and value themselves enabled me to overcome my reluctance and share my story.

Chapter 1

My book begins as my life did, with my parents. It made sense that they were drawn to each other. My mother was stunningly beautiful, highly intelligent, and multi-talented. She demanded attention, and knew how to use her "womanly wiles" to charm a man. Mom told me that she was desperate to have a child and would go to any lengths to do so. My biological father, as she described him, was charismatic, resourceful, creative, and successful. Most importantly to my mother, he was capable of procreating, as evidenced by his children from a prior marriage. With my birth, my mother had literally brought to life the goal to which much of her adult existence had been devoted. She had envisioned her role of mother as integral to a loving, traditional family. Sadly, she had been abandoned both by her family of origin and her husband.

In her memoir, excerpted later in this book, my mother revealed that she had a great deal of experience with adversity. Her nature and early environment led her to take full responsibility for the situation in which we found ourselves. As early as possible, she determined which areas of our lives she could control and, in doing so, manage more efficiently. Once I was "independent," she could reclaim a measure of freedom. This had the obvious benefit of releasing her from unpleasant and messy child-rearing tasks. The drive to control herself and others, particularly me, caused conflict between us through the years. The following anecdote sheds light on a dominant aspect of my mother's personality.

When I was a few months old, she initiated toilet training. My mother insisted that she had accomplished this task. She was unconvinced by the pediatrician's explanation that she had simply learned when to place me on the potty! Unfortunately for all concerned, I was a "late bloomer" in this regard, whether due to rebellion or developmental delay. However, at a very early age, I learned that being unable to meet unrealistic, unachievable goals would be met with disparagement. Worse yet were my fears of punishment or even abandonment. Even as a toddler, I would go to great lengths to prevent mom's detection of my failures, as the following anecdote reveals. My mother had reconciled with her sister Etta, who had been very opposed to mom's marriage. We were visiting my beloved aunt,who lived in a rural area of Ulster County, in upper New York state. The sisters took every opportunity to enjoy their time together. This freedom from supervision left me to my own devices. I used those occasions to hide the evidence of my "accidents." "Mommy will be very mad at me for my dirty underpants," I thought. "I have to hide them." After our visit, Aunt Etta would find "buried treasure" in her soil. Perhaps her beloved garden was particularly fruitful, after my summer "fertilization forays."

While I showed indications of creative problem-solving abilities, these usually had unfortunate, unforeseen consequences. This meant that, apart from ethical considerations, I was discouraged early on from engaging in a life of crime! Once, when I was presumably napping in my crib at my aunt's home, my mother and Aunt Etta came into the guest bedroom and found shattered glass in a photo on top of the bureau. As was usually the case, my aunt pointed the finger of accusation at me. My mother was incredulous; Etta had truly gone too far this time. "Really Etta, that is ridiculous. How could she possibly have been responsible for that damage?"

Aunt Etta sweetly asked, "Marlene darling, how did you get Aunt Etta's picture?" I happily showed her, by climbing out of my crib and pulling out the bureau's drawers to create a makeshift ladder. This incident was neither the first nor the last of my misadventures. Curious about the anatomy of dolls, I would conduct surgical dismemberments of various parts of their bodies. Unfortunately, my babies had inevitably become amputees once the surgeries were completed.

While certain of my childish adventures may have amused my mother, she was exhausted by my almost ceaseless activities. By day's end, mom was usually looking forward to relaxing with her friends or relatives. She would go quite far to gain a little peace and quiet. While on a visit to Etta, she and some family members were playing a card game. To ensure that there would be no interruptions, a dire warning from a "witch" was broadcast into my bedroom, from my aunt's intercom system. "Do not dare be a naughty girl and climb out of your bed." I lay frozen in my crib, and the adults were assured that there would be no disruptions to their enjoyment. During the mid-1940s, the ramifications of that warning to a child who already was terrified of catastrophic consequences for the slightest, unintended misbehavior, did not (as far as I could tell) occur to my mother or any of the others.

As I developed, my increasingly independent actions created new opportunities for my behavior to reflect my undiagnosed neurological deficits. These, in turn, resulted in additional frustrations for me and my mother. As she saw in me a reflection of herself, each day was a fresh chance to present me to the world as picture perfect. The late forties model girl was clean, neat, careful and quiet. I can still hear my mother saying to me, "Modulate your voice." This was usually followed by "Cleanliness is next to Godliness." Unfortunately, the image she attempted to create was doomed to failure. Despite my best efforts to be a good girl, within mere minutes some dirt or rip would appear on my body, clothing, or both. Even worse, I was unaware and uncaring about my appearance. It did not help that I was a tomboy. I relished sandbox architecture and preferred adventurous outdoor games to "playing house," which bored me. Finally, many household objects became victims of my curiosity, poor coordination and imbalance. My hard handling of upstate New York's sensitive plumbing fixtures was particularly troublesome, as I could not be banned from using these essential utilities! Aunt Etta used to describe me as "Marlene with the *delacatka hentalach* (delicate hands)."

Not to be denied her chance to bask vicariously in the limelight, my mother took every opportunity to display my precocious verbal skills. On command, I could sing the many Russian ballads I had been taught and recite any number of verses. As I was not permitted to be out of her sight before I gave my performances, she could ensure that I would be presentable.

It was difficult to recognize and deal with the interdependence that arose between my mother and me. I believe that this is often true in single parent/single child relationships. The emotional insecurities that plagued my mother, despite her gifts, drove her to mold me into a daughter who would love her unconditionally, be the best possible reflection of her, and be there to care for her in the future. When my mother said, "It is you and I against the world," she literally meant it. A poem she wrote as a member of a senior citizen's creative writing class movingly illuminates her ambivalent feelings.

CROSSROADS

The iron gate closed with a clanging sound
echoing the pang in my heart.
She rushed through the gate to join the children,
lined up two by two, led into the building,
swallowed up like Jonah in the belly of the whale.
Not once did she turn back to wave,
knowing I'd be there to see all went well.
Her first day at school
was my partial freedom from responsibility.
I stood by the gate for a while
emotions swept over me like a tidal wave.
Her new world would consist of relationships,
experiences in which I would have no part.
The turbulence started to subside.
I felt myself drifting,
allowing the current to guide me
through uncharted waters ahead.

Chapter 2

A command of the language was of great importance to my mother, a child of immigrant parents who prided herself on being articulate. As mentioned earlier, she was exceedingly proud that I developed language skills at a very young age. I remember my mother saying, "I cannot wait until you read by yourself," thereby freeing her from that task. Fortunately, I was able to master this skill well before entering kindergarten. I had a very active imagination, and books allowed me to expand beyond the usual confines of my life, to escape, to laugh, and to share experiences with others. My mother and I shared a bedroom and the only private area was a walk-in closet that served as my reading room. Our budget was limited so only school texts were purchased for me. Furthermore, mom said that it was wasteful to buy me pleasurable books as I finished them too quickly. However, as we often frequented the public library, I always had a good selection to choose from. It was a great advantage, early in life, to develop strong reading capabilities. I have derived many academic, professional and personal benefits from this. However, it would have filled an enormous emotional void in me if my mother had read to me when I was a youngster.

I spent my childhood vacations and summers in Kingston, New York, the city where my mother was born, and in rural Ulster County. My Aunt Etta and her husband Bill ran a summer bungalow colony in Ulster Park. The colony was situated next to beautiful Mirror Lake. Aunt Etta and Uncle Bill had two sons. The elder, Herbert, had been institutionalized with a progressive neurological disorder, many years prior to my birth. Etta and Bill visited him each weekend. When I was a toddler in their charge, I was included in their trips. As was the case with other family secrets, I was not encouraged to seek an explanation about the origin of his condition. However, I did understand that it was progressive. I was fearful that I too might develop the same condition, deteriorate, and be hospitalized in adulthood. Their second son, my dear Cousin Bernie, was a successful owner of a Firestone store in Kingston. He was well known, respected, and politically active in the area. The front of his large store contained many items, some of which were toys. The rear carried new tires and older ones that were retread and repaired. (For this reason, I feel nostalgic when smelling burning rubber at an auto shop.) Bernie was married to Eleanor and had one daughter, Sherry, who is 18 months younger than I. My Cousin Bernie always treated me like a daughter, and Sherry and I were like sisters. (Only in adulthood did I have the maturity to consider that Sherry might have felt ambivalent about sharing her parents with this ephemeral sister.) We were frequently taken to the store, where I was in awe of the wealth of goods surrounding me. One of my fondest memories is of the Christmas when Cousin Bernie surprised Sherry and me with beautiful, full-sized doll carriages that I proudly wheeled around my Brooklyn neighborhood. The knowledge that my cousin was the owner of his store conferred a pride by association and a feeling of security in belonging to the Singer family.

Given my mother's objections, circuses, parks and the like were generally taboo. Amusement parks were also precluded, with the exception of occasional merry-go-round rides. They were acceptable to my mother, and were the only ride I could tolerate because of my severe motion sickness. Unfortunately, my mother had no option but to include me as a passenger in our car. Until I developed further, there would be a predictable eruption after every ride. She cleaned our upholstery, muttering her displeasure, while I cringed in fear and shame. Cousin Bernie did not have my mother's budgetary constraints, nor was he disgusted by play times that could be noisy, stinky or dirty. Sherry and I enjoyed all the activities that delighted children. There were pony rides, Easter egg hunts, a visit to the "North Pole," unlimited trips to Johnny's frankfurter stand, Stewart's self-served ice cream sundaes, and so much more. I also erupted in Cousin Bernie's car while traveling to our destinations. However, he took this in stride, and therefore, so did I.

I enjoyed time with other relatives who spent summers in the bungalow colony, or in nearby Kingston. Annie was a cousin somewhat younger than Sherry, and she often spent days with us. Her beauty was evident, even when she was a young child. I recall that two adolescent boys on the grounds were charmed by her appearance. Observing their reaction underscored the importance of beauty for a female. Annie's grandparents shared the bungalow with her older brother, Freddie, and her mother, Eleanor. Her father, Herb, drove up each weekend. Everyone in our small community referred to Annie's grandparents by their Yiddish names, Bubbie and Zadie. They were, in word and deed, everyone's grandparents. As I had no biological grandparents, their affection for and inclusion of me in family occasions provided support, security and a belief that I was lovable. I also had great fun playing in the Kingston woods behind Richie and Bobbie Fertel's home. I recall that our mothers briefly tied Rich and me to the trees so they could rest and prevent us from inadvertently causing harm to each other.

While my happiest memories are of days spent in Kingston, I retain certain painful recollections of them. Although my Aunt Etta, like my mother, was anxious about many things, she had the primary responsibility for running the bungalow colony. This kept her occupied most of the day, leaving me unsupervised. As the oldest of three female cousins, I was expected to demonstrate "leadership skills," and to set a good example. This was always my intention, and of course, I was expected to plan some novel and exciting activity. My lack of maturity and foresight invariably led to problems. My mother often heard tales of Marlene's incredible escapades. Annie and Sherry, as well as my friends, fulfilled the image and expectations for young girls in the early 1950s. They were quiet, neat, orderly, and careful with their belongings and those of others. My contemporaries were generally happy "playing house" or other sedentary games, or following the suggestions of our elders. As noted earlier, I, on the other hand, always pushed the proverbial envelope, but acted in complete innocence. Never did I anticipate the inevitable disasters that resulted from my childish spirit of adventure.

One anecdote that was well known in our family illustrates my somewhat unique childhood experiences. I thought that it might be fun to explore the other side of Mirror Lake, but neglected to mention this plan to my aunt. Unbeknownst to us, a convict had escaped from a local prison the evening before our walk. We were gone for several hours before my Cousin Bernie located us. We were happily picking apples from an orchard on the other side of the lake. Imagine my surprise at the greeting I received as lead explorer. "Oh my G-d. I made my aunt spit blood!" Despite scoldings from my Aunt Etta and Cousin Bernie, I always felt their unconditional love and barely disguised amusement and pride in my activities. Experiencing this would have an impact on my parenting so many years later.

As is true in everyone's life, wonderful times are interspersed with times of unhappiness and fear. All our family members were deeply saddened by the tragic illness that befell our Cousin Eleanor. She developed a very severe form of multiple sclerosis in her early 30s, and bravely challenged her weakening faculties. I recall that Sherry and I watched as it took her mother an incredibly long time, with the use of a walker, to visit a neighbor across the street. We were able to provide some assistance in the early years of the disorder. But after a while, there was little we could do.

Chapter 3

My life and sense of identity in Ulster Park and Kingston were very different from what I experienced while living with my mother in Brooklyn, New York. I was the only child in my neighborhood who did not have a father. I lived with the constant fear that my mother would fail to be there for me when I arrived home from school. Mom would often say, "I want to go to a desert island and be alone." When angry, she would refuse to speak to me for extended periods of time; I rarely knew what I had done to be punished with isolation. In contrast to my experiences and feelings about Kingston, my mother often expressed her intense dislike of small town life. She recalled that "everybody knows your business and gossips about you." She told me that her mother had warned her about the dangers of New York City. However, her dreams of an exciting career as a torch singer in a nightclub could not be fulfilled in Kingston.

When I was about eight years old, it was decided that a more structured summer program would be beneficial. I spent every season at a sleep-away camp through my mid-teens. In the early years, I was always eager to go. However, once I settled into my bunk, a profound homesickness afflicted me. That, and great difficulty with all sports, led me to call my mother. "Mommy, I'm so lonely and I miss you so much. Please pick me up and let me come home." My request was always denied. Her voice tinged with annoyance and weariness, mom warned, "Being home will be boring. I won't chauffeur you to friends and events. You made a decision, I paid for the camping season and you must accept the consequences. More importantly, you have to learn to deal with difficult situations. If you accept defeat now, you will be unprepared for the challenges you will face as an adult." Hearing this, I scolded myself for making another bad decision. "I should have known better." I also understood that mom needed and deserved a break from her ongoing mothering duties. While her words were very painful at the time, that advice has served me well. (Ironically, I have drawn upon that wisdom in the ongoing battles to see myself as capable of making decisions independently from my mother.) Lonely, I wrote to Aunt Etta, whose bungalow colony was nearby. My repeated pleading for her and Uncle Bill to visit were met with various excuses, which were hurtful and puzzling. Aunt Etta was also very reluctant to answer my letters, as she felt deep shame at her phonetic spelling. I continued to implore her and she did eventually respond. I have kept those notes, which I treasure. At the end of the season, my mother drove to the camp to take me home. As we sat in the car, she told me that Uncle Bill had suddenly died of a heart attack, at the beginning of the summer.

Although devastated by her husband's death, Aunt Etta continued to run the bungalow colony for a while longer. I was profoundly influenced by the strength and capabilities of my mother and her sisters. I had been told about the hardships the immigrants had endured in Russia, which further engendered my admiration and respect. As for my Aunt Etta, Uncle Bill's death was yet another loss in a life marked by great adversity. This began at her birth, in a small town on the eventual border between Russia and Poland. As Jews, the family was subject to frequent pogroms (violence). Her father made seven trips across the ocean, taking his wife and then each child separately. Although he was the owner of a brush factory, he had to leave behind most of his belongings. Therefore, they arrived in Kingston with no knowledge of the language, scarce goods, and very limited funds. It was decided that the children would complete their education and learn English. Etta was a teenager and she and her siblings were embarrassed to be in a class with young children, so my grandfather managed to secure informal tutoring. As a young adult, Etta married Bill, an American from a prominent family, and adapted well to her new country and position.

Another aunt, Pearl, was widowed with six children, and ran a small supermarket in Kingston. Aunt Pearl delighted in telling everyone who would listen that as a youngster, "Marlene asked a group of her playmates to help themselves to anything in her store. It's all free!" Unlike many of my peers in the late 1940s and early 1950s, the females in my family were successfully engaged in the marketplace. Therefore, I have had confidence that women can handle themselves well in business. This has had an enduring effect on my preferences in professional relationships. When given the choice, I generally select a woman to provide professional services. My mother, of a prior generation than mine, viewed men as authority figures and was puzzled by my perspective. She maintained this despite my admiration at her accomplishments in the workforce, and her belief about the importance of women being financially independent. Even mom's great pride in my academic and professional achievements did not alter her views.

Unfortunately, the strength of my mothers' siblings in business did not hold true for their health. My Uncle Bill was the first to go. My mother's other, considerably older siblings then died over successive summers. My mother was a firm believer in allowing children to experience the fundamental realities of life, so I accompanied her to family funerals. While most of my peers recall weekends spent enjoying traditional outings with family, many of my memories are of frequent trips to the cemetery. In addition to attending funerals, I accompanied my mother and her oldest sister, Jeanette, on their cemetery visits. Aunt Jeanette was in excellent health, and was, in fact, "a polar bear." She had commissioned a bench to be built in front of her family's tombstone. We would sit there while Aunt Jeanette made my mother promise: "Visit my grave and tell me what that butcher's daughter is doing to my beloved son." At a young age, I began to understand that the instinct to protect your child may extend even beyond your death. Being a single parent, my mother alone had to make important decisions about when and how to present the realities of life to me. These experiences have had a profound impact on my entire life.

As I matured, the realities of life and my world continued to shape me as a complex individual with many thoughts and emotions. The growing awareness of my mortality terrified me. My first experience of this intense fear occurred while I was at summer camp. I discovered a lump on the back of my neck and checked it daily, trying to calm myself. "Should I tell someone? Is it cancer?" When I finally reported it, my parents were called. They traveled a very long distance to the camp and an even longer distance to the nearest town to have me examined. The growth was diagnosed as a swollen lymph node, which needed no attention. While I was tremendously relieved, new concerns arose. "What if other growths appear in the future?" I was afraid of my own fear, of not being able to distinguish perfectly normal bodily features from the abnormal ones. This preoccupation itself seemed abnormal, as I compared myself to my bunkmates. The doubts that all youngsters have about their ability to handle increasing responsibilities of maturity were intensified by my concerns. The belief that I could not trust my judgment in vital matters pertaining to me and others who are dependent upon me has had an enormous impact on every area of my life. This belief allows only two options - both of which are intolerable. One is that I am totally dependent on others, who I believe are capable, responsible and trustworthy. That option would be burdensome to me and to those upon whom I would be excessively dependent. The other option would have me faced with decisions that I feel I am incapable of making. This would then either paralyze me with doubt or have me tortured by the belief that my judgement is inevitably faulty. There is a great deal of literature about the difficulties with "locus of control" in the learning-disabled population. An individual having an "internal locus of control" is defined as an emotionally healthy person, who sees him- or herself as the appropriate source of actions and consequences, both positive and negative. In contrast, the "external locus of control" individual projects outwards from him- or herself to other sources in regard to decisions, actions and effects.

My neurological deficits were progressively manifesting themselves as I faced growing expectations appropriate to my developmental stages. I was fearless when faced with many activities children, and even adults, found challenging. In contrast, I was paralyzed with fear when first standing at the top of an escalator. I refused to get on it for many months. "Why are they (other children) not afraid of these dangerous rolling stairs?" The fact that I lacked some capability, that I had such difficulty doing what everyone else could readily handle, was itself terrifying. My mother tried bribing me with goodies and my favorite television shows. Initially, those very desirable treats were not sufficient to move me. However, the fear of my mother's disapproval was stronger than the fear of injuries I imagined I would suffer. Eventually, with a pounding heart, and sweaty hands grasping the sides, I stepped on. While I have braved many escalators, there is still always a moment of hesitation and an impulse to turn away.

My mother and I lived in a one-bedroom apartment. Although we slept in twin beds, rarely did I go to sleep feeling secure. She dated often, and left me in the care of a series of babysitters, who failed to be captured by my charms. They couldn't be bothered to check under my bed or in the closet to see if there was a witch or boogeyman hiding in there. They were too busy going through my mother's closets and drawers. When they finished, I would be warned, "Do not tell your mom." She was fascinating and glamorous to these teens whose stay-at-home mothers were found wanting by comparison. Each time mom went out, I was terrified that she would die in an accident or leave me forever, and no family member would be willing to care for me. Statements she made when tired or exasperated fueled these fears. As I previously wrote, mom would say that she couldn't stand to be confined, would wish aloud that she could go to some desert island, and, like Greta Garbo, just wanted to be left alone. When she became angry, she would not speak to me for extended periods. Often, I had no idea what I had done or failed to do to provoke her. These statements and actions could be expected and understood as momentary expressions of exhaustion and frustration from a single parent with virtually no support, even from one who was insightful and experienced with children. However, as a child, I could not understand her perspective. Exacerbating my fears was the orphanage that stood across the street from the primary school I attended. I imagined myself being placed there. Night after night, huddled in bed with my dolls, I acted out an escape fantasy, where my babies and I managed to flee to a safe and happy home. It never occurred to me that this was unusual or unhealthy. Given my circumstances, it could be anticipated.

My mother's ambivalent needs and perspectives about our relationship resulted in my being overprotected on certain occasions, while at other times I was encouraged to act with a great deal of freedom. This liberty was unusual, even in the fifties. The resulting confusion further undermined my confidence in anticipating what was expected of me and acting accordingly. Boundaries could not be firmly established. Early in my childhood, mom repeatedly stressed the need for me to be able to care for myself, "should something happen to me." Of course, this further exacerbated my already great fear of abandonment. Overwhelmed with dread, I begged her for reassurance. This was provided by her promise that "I will live until a ripe old age," which I knew could be beyond her ability to keep. However, I also understood that I should not express disbelief. When mom emphasized the importance of my being honest and trustworthy, I became confused in addition to being frightened. She explained that the only permissible exception to complete honesty would be to spare someone's feelings. Mom warned me to "Confess your wrongdoing upfront. Withholding the truth or lying will result in a greater punishment, once you are found guilty." Punishment could not be avoided, regardless of whether the act had been the result of an accident or intentional. I was determined to be as careful as possible, and to accept the inevitable consequences of my failures.

Having been instructed in the importance of being prepared, I believed that I was ready to care for myself. My mother's plan to accomplish this was for me to take the public bus to Brooklyn's busy shopping center and spend my Saturdays there. I was given some money to have lunch at Woolworth's Five and Ten and do a little shopping. I was supremely confident as I set out. Since none of my peers were given this "privilege," I believed it indicated my mother's special trust in me. I really enjoyed my Saturdays. Fortunately, I was not faced with any situation that a child of my limited experience and maturity could not handle. Upon coming home, I showed my mother what I had purchased (and sometimes shoplifted) and glowed when she praised me.

My Saturday excursions had prepared me for solo long-distance travel to Kingston. My mother would take me to the Port Authority bus terminal in Manhattan. I would eagerly board the Greyhound bus and happily chatter away to whatever adult was in the adjoining seat, anticipating being with my beloved relatives. On one occasion, the bus broke down in a snowstorm. Not nonplussed in the least, I asked the driver to "Please call my Uncle Bill. He is waiting for me and will be worried if I am late." My family was amazed that I had the presence of mind at age seven to take this action. Frankly, today, I am too. It has been these inconsistencies which made it so difficult to predict my behaviors and take appropriate action.

As I previously wrote, my mother prided herself on being prepared and in control of every circumstance that could arise. She almost always was, throughout her long life. Therefore, it is noteworthy that she was unprepared for an inevitable conversation with me. Mom told me that when I was a youngster, an encyclopedia salesman came to our door. In an attempt to quickly end the conversation, she told him that she did not have a husband. Apparently, that was all the opportunity I needed to ask what had been on my mind. "Where is my daddy?" Thinking quickly, she told me that my father died in the war. (She did not recant that story until I confronted her with it some twenty years later.) Interestingly, I have very little memory of that conversation or of any thoughts I had regarding her truthfulness. That was the only occasion during which I gave voice to the questions I had about my father. This silence was in contrast to my great curiosity about the world around and within me. As I grew, I apparently accepted the absence of any pictures of my father, his family, and the lack of paternal family contact. On the occasions when my mother did reference him, it was by his first name, "Manny." She would say, "I shouldn't have married him. He is divorced and has children from that union." That was followed by, "It is better to have no father than a bad father." Mom would then always emphasize that she encouraged him to visit his sons and daughter. I would rush to reassure her, saying, "You did nothing wrong by marrying him." Amazingly, this decades-long conspiracy of silence, which included my mother's entire family and friends, was never breached. Nevertheless, on a subliminal level, it was yet another shameful aspect of my being that set me apart from other youngsters.

Given the secrecy and shame I associated with my origin and parentage, I took the yearly celebration of my birth very much to heart. As money has been limited for most of my life, the cost of the gifts or lavishness of the party was not at all important to me. The "surprise" cake and card, along with whoever else was present, temporarily dispelled the constant doubts that my very existence was not worthwhile or good. However, the validation I sought, on a less than fully conscious level, was from contact with my biological father. Once my mother remarried, I felt guilty for even having the wish, given how wonderful my adoptive father was. However, as is the case with many adopted children, there is an intense curiosity and drive for information and connection. (I still feel a pang when I see a young girl at play with her father, and perceive the security and joy she radiates while being held by the first man to whom she will give and from whom she will receive love. As an adult, I understand that it is no longer possible to recapture those childhood moments, nor fill the void by finding my biological father. These experiences and my misdiagnoses have impelled me to know as much about myself as possible. That dedication eventually extended to my professional life. As I previously wrote, it was extremely difficult for me to obtain my doctorate. However, I intended to be as well trained as possible to provide the service deserved and needed by students with learning and attentional disorders. The doctorate also confers credibility. I believed it increased the probability of having my views given serious consideration in the professional community and becoming an agent for change.)

As was true of most young girls growing up in the fifties, I was expected to develop expertise in household management skills. This would prepare me for marriage. My mother had excellent culinary abilities. She would firmly lecture me, saying, "It is a wife's duty to have a nutritious and delicious meal for her husband when he returns from work." (Once remarried, she did so every day of my father's life and virtually nothing was allowed to interfere with this.) When I was a young girl, I marveled at these abilities, just as I did about all her other skills. Cooking seemed to be so much fun; it was an activity that we could do together, and during which we made wonderful meals. However, although I don't remember my efforts, I recall my mother wearily saying, "I am just too tired to clean up your mess. You will have to learn in your own kitchen after you marry."

Chapter 4

Once I began school, academic difficulties surfaced. I had trouble controlling my "chattering" with other classmates. I forgot books, assignments, papers to be signed, and other things. My homework tended to get crumpled, with illegible handwriting, and was often spotted with something (as was I). Simple arithmetic was proving to be troublesome. It was also becoming clear that distinguishing my left from my right was not coming naturally. Finally, I had very little natural grace or athletic ability, although I had a great deal of energy. However, I could read very well, understand, and articulate what I had read at an advanced level.

When I began elementary school, my mother took a part-time job as a secretary for a social worker in Hometerm court, and loved her job. It was somewhat unusual during that period to have a working mother, and one who attended adult education classes in psychology, considered an esoteric subject in our circle. I was exceedingly proud of my beautiful, smart, sophisticated mother, who introduced me to this fascinating field. Unfortunately, a little knowledge proved to be a dangerous thing. Freudian theory was fashionable at the time. My mother was instructed in some of the basic tenets. She then felt comfortable interpreting my behaviors, as well as those of other people, according to Freud's theories. As the years passed, my as yet undiagnosed symptoms of learning disabilities and attentional disorders continued to manifest themselves. Mom interpreted them as expressing some form of unconscious resistance or hostility towards her. For example, when we went shopping and I trailed behind her, I frequently stepped on the backs of her shoes. She would then accuse me of doing this intentionally. The motive, mom believed, was my jealousy of her shapely legs! (In fact, the causes were perceptual distortions, as well as poor balance and coordination.) Sadly, her interpretations resulted in my questioning the most innocent of my stumbles.

Not surprisingly, I proved frustrating to my teachers. "Underachieving, sloppy, careless, and scatterbrained," were the terms used to describe me. My mother was frequently called to school to hear about my chatting with classmates and my uneven scholastic performance. I remember burning with shame at my inability to accomplish what my teachers insisted I could do, if only I would try. I desperately wanted to please my mother, to have her be as proud of me as I was of her. However, no amount of effort on my part was met with success. As my personal and academic struggles continued, I was about to confront a new set of life-altering challenges.

During my early childhood, my mother dated several men, each for an extended period, before meeting the man she eventually married. I only have a limited memory of one of these men. He obviously had not read the literature, which stressed the importance of winning over the child of the desirable divorcee. He often scolded me, saying that

I was causing my mother much heartache by my various misdeeds. I responded by telling her, "I do not want him to be my daddy." Fortunately, that relationship ended. However, the search continued, as my mother very much wanted a partner for life. Both of us wanted a father for me, who would provide love and acceptance.

When I was about seven, my mother persuaded Aunt Etta to take care of me, so that she could vacation in Florida. Mom hoped to bring home more than a suntan and souvenirs. Convinced of the importance of the mission, my aunt was persuaded. Once mom was there and looking gorgeous, she attracted the attention of an admirer. She found him charming, but too young to be her partner. This fellow told her that he knew a widower, a colleague, who might be a more appropriate suitor. My mother had to board her plane before this gentleman was available to meet her. It seemed that the opportunity would not present itself. However, her plane was grounded and she was unable to make other arrangements. They met, and – the rest is history. She thanked G-d as well as saying it was "*beshart*," the Yiddish word for fate. While this was transpiring, my aunt, an intensely private person, was explaining to me why it was inappropriate to confide to bus companions that my mother was going to Florida to find a husband.

When my father and I met, it was love at first sight. Al Charney was gentle, kind, generous, had a sense of humor, intelligent, and always saw the good in me. When he said, "Malke [my Yiddish name], you always look beautiful to me," he meant it. While I had no reservations about him, my parents had the maturity to understand that it was going to be very difficult to blend two families. My father had two daughters from his previous marriage, one five years and one ten years older than I. At the time of my parents' meeting, my father had been a widower for only about a year. His wife had a heart condition that progressively worsened after the birth of their second child. Understandably, he needed time before committing himself to a serious relationship, and to help his children deal with the loss of their mother. He and my mother began dating on their return from Florida. After a considerable period of time had elapsed and my father continued to waver about a commitment, my mother took action. The following summer, she vacationed in the town where my father's daughters were camp counselors, and invited them to her hotel for dinner. When they arrived, she introduced them to her new male escort, an affluent dentist who was obviously very interested in her. When my mother returned home, she found my father on bended knee with a large, beautiful engagement ring. As I wrote earlier, my mother was a firm believer in fate. However, there are circumstances where, she would tell you, her timely intervention was critical.

I was thrilled at the announcement of my parents' engagement. At age eight, I did not have much experience in hosting a bridal shower, nor did I have any peers to consult. Nevertheless, I wanted this to be a very special surprise. I invited all of my friends and asked them to contribute their money for shower gifts. I then went to Woolworth's where I purchased items appropriate for the bride to be, and a cake. On the day of the event, I gave each person a bowl filled with a mixture of flour and rice. When my mother came home from work, we jumped out from our hiding places and "showered" her. We then presented our gifts and intended to have cake with the guest of honor. However, my mother was so distressed about the rice mixture on the floor that she wouldn't or couldn't join us. My friends and I ate the cake while she vacuumed around us, and then they went home. I had ruined a once-in-a-lifetime day. Instead of pleasing my mother, I had disappointed, perhaps even angered her. I would have to try harder. But often, something I neglected to account for would result in failure, humiliation, perplexity, frustration and pain.

Shortly after their wedding, my father expressed his commitment to adopt me. This meant that he would be legally responsible for me, as if he were a biological parent. On the day of adoption, the judge asked me if I wanted to be adopted. Eagerly I said, "I do." At first, it was a little awkward to call him daddy. That was a word I had never spoken and a relationship I had never experienced. However, after a short time, my mother said that she wanted me to address him that way. It quickly felt right, and from then on he was my father, in word and deed.

As for my parents' union, the course of true love never runs smoothly. This is particularly true in a "blended" marriage, where children are involved. During my parent's engagement, my mother was advised, by members of my father's family, that Deborah, the younger of his two daughters, was most likely going to prove a challenge. This was an accurate prediction. Her mother had been an invalid and died when the youngster was approaching puberty. My mother and I moved into my father's two-bedroom row home in Brooklyn when they returned from their honeymoon. For the first six months, I slept on the living room couch. My older step sister, Adrianne, married shortly after my parents did, and moved nearby. When she married, I moved into the bedroom that the two sisters shared. Not surprisingly, this did not prove to be a good arrangement. I was desperate to earn my new sister's approval and, ultimately, her love. She was a teenager, and to have a relationship with an older sister was very desirable. Then too, she was a very good student and had many talents, which I greatly admired. Both sisters had taken piano lessons, and the younger one also had vocal instruction. My mother had learned to play the piano by ear, and very much enjoyed accompanying herself. When we moved into my father's home, the one item that came with us was the piano that my mother had saved for, over the course of many years. My father played the flute. Given that we were a musical family, and my mother believed that playing the piano would be rewarding for me, she engaged a teacher. Practice demanded a concentration I did not have. After months of my repeatedly interrupting her during short bouts of practice, my mother uncharacteristically had an emotional meltdown. She grabbed my hair and dragged me into the next room, screaming, "Marlene, I cannot stand your behavior. There will be no more lessons!" While I was relieved with that decision, I was shocked and pained by what she did and said. I had driven her to the proverbial end of her rope, and could not share what was so meaningful to her, as my step sisters could.

In addition to sharing her love of music, my mother felt great empathy for Deborah. Mom had lost her own mother at an early age. She shared with me that my grandfather had briefly become involved with a woman, sometime after his wife's death. Mom revealed her refusal to accept such a relationship. Although she was deeply pained when Deborah physically or verbally abused me, she did not take a stand against her, both out of empathy and for other reasons. As much as my father loved me, he too was unable or unwilling to discipline his daughter, although he knew I did not deserve her treatment. Without my father's support, my mother felt that as a stepparent, she could not act. She told me, "You must be more understanding than she. The loss of a mother is more devastating than the absence of a father in a daughter's formative years." My mother also attempted to limit opportunities for Deborah to feel that I was being favored. When a new article of clothing was purchased for me, it was placed in the bottom of a drawer for a while, and then incorporated into my wardrobe. All of this had the effect of eroding my trust in those closest to me. Furthermore, it fostered my belief that other people's needs were more important than mine.

Chapter 5

As I indicated earlier, mathematics was a subject in which I always needed help. Deborah and her boyfriend, Marc, both of whom were very adept in mathematics, had been enlisted to provide tutoring. However, neither had the patience or the knowledge of how to convey the concepts to me. Another family member, who was skilled in the subject, volunteered as a tutor. At first, I felt great frustration and shame about my difficulty in grasping the subject matter. However, Neil was patient, and had a great ability to instruct me. I began to relax and focus on the material. Hope slowly began to grow that I could master the subject. However, over the course of our sessions, I began to be aware that his hands were traveling upwards, toward my breasts. Since I had frequently been told that I was naïve, and had faulty judgment, my initial response was to shift my body and tell myself that nothing was wrong. However, one evening when we were alone in my home, he pinned me to the wall and molested me. As he had a violent temper when provoked, I was terrified, and did not resist. I reported what had happened to my mother as soon as she returned home. To my shock, she didn't think that it was much more than "boys will be boys." She counseled me not to disclose the incident to his wife, for fear it would ruin their marriage. Mom advised me to avoid being alone with him. This was difficult, given the nature of our relationship. However, other than one or two petrifying incidents, I managed to get through it. I did not tell my father, and do not remember why I decided not to. A few possibilities have occurred to me. Perhaps I was embarrassed, felt that he would not act, or was fearful that he would confront this "monster" and be harmed. The experience has caused many flashbacks and painful emotions through the years. Trust in my mother and myself was damaged. My body was violated. I was treated as an object, disrespected, and became ambivalent about being seen as attractive or welcoming. At times I believed my appearance was an advantage and at other times it seemed to represent a threat to me. As was common in the late fifties, it would have been unthinkable for me to reveal the molestation and lack of parental support to any other family member or close friend. Fortunately, the healthy love of my brother-in-law Marc, Cousin Bernie, and father lessened the trauma of my being molested. These relationships ultimately enabled me to establish normal relationships with the opposite sex.

Despite withholding from everyone what I had endured, I was able to make friends easily. However, a major problem arose, when a parent offered to drive me home after a friend and I had spent some time together. It was extremely difficult for me to provide directions to and from my home, even when I was a short distance away. When being driven home from some activity, I struggled to guide the parent to my door; I felt humiliated, and was drenched in sweat by the time I arrived at my destination. Similarly, I had difficulty distinguishing between the streets on either side of my house. We lived in the middle of the block, between Avenues A and B. My mother was puzzled and said, "Marlene, for the life of me, I cannot understand why you continually confuse the two."

As for the time spent in school, family dynamics were exacerbating my academic challenges. While I was an elementary school student, I was administered a statewide aptitude battery. The results showed a significant discrepancy between my verbal and mathematical/spatial abilities. Nevertheless, the testing indicated that my capacity for mathematics was significantly greater than what I was achieving in the classroom. A meeting between my parents and the school psychologist was scheduled. It was agreed that my emotional functioning should be assessed. I was very frightened by the content of a number of questions. One item asked if I would attend an execution if I had the choice? "My God, what do they think is wrong with me?" My underachievement and poor performance were subsequently attributed to the stress I was experiencing at the melding of two families. I don't recall any suggestions on how to improve the family situation. However, I had a series of professional math tutors through the years. I recall one incident very clearly. As a high school student, I was required to pass a statewide Regents examination in geometry. My parents had engaged a teacher from my school to assist me. After our final session, as Mr. Rosenthal turned to leave, he stopped, paused, and said, "Well, at least you're cute!" I panicked, fearing that I would never earn my high school diploma.

Fortunately, I did manage to squeak by in geometry, but I still have nightmares about that course.

As I progressed through high school, the difficulties I experienced continued to be attributed to a number of factors. One was family dynamics. Another was that girls generally were not expected to be proficient in mathematics. A third was my raging teenage hormones. Until my junior year, when I began to be concerned about college, I wasn't particularly interested in my studies. I found them either boring or frustrating. My parents expected me to earn a college degree. That was considered the appropriate completion of my education. This would enable me to be a well-rounded partner for my future husband, serving the function of a "finishing school." I also had to be prepared to support myself, should the need arise. My parents expressed their view that a teaching position would accomplish these goals. I did not support that career choice for at least two reasons. I felt very uncomfortable when imagining myself interacting with an entire classroom of students. More important, however, was my continuing fascination with the field of psychology. There was a reason, beyond my academic interest, that led me to major in the discipline. The love for my Aunt Etta, and empathy with her pain at Herbert's neurological disorder, institutionalization and subsequent death, were powerful motivators. I intended to research and treat brain disorders. I planned to earn a doctorate in psychology, as well as to marry and raise a family.

However, I gave little thought to what marriage and child rearing would entail. I had very few opportunities to care for younger family members and did not seek out positions. On a few occasions, I was asked to babysit for a family member's child and found it very anxiety-provoking. I attributed the feeling to inexperience, but that was the result, not the cause of my hesitancy. Being responsible for a young child, who was very active and unable to communicate much verbally, was terrifying! I felt I wasn't sufficiently prepared to be responsible for the child's life. In truth, I was ambivalent about obtaining any job. At the suggestion of applying for a job, I felt subliminal threat and dread. I knew only that there would be unexplainable errors. Without a clear understanding of what I was feeling and why, I could neither articulate nor justify my reluctance to venture forth. Although my parents did not need me to provide income, my mother believed that work experience would prepare me for later employment. I agreed with the argument, and desperately wanted to succeed, for myself and for them. Once again, I felt shame and pain at disappointing my parents.

Similarly, although I longed for the freedom that driving would allow, the thought of myself driving a car was overwhelming. My mother stressed, "You must learn to drive. Driving is essential to your independence and functioning as an adult." She very much enjoyed driving and was very good at it, despite her poor sense of direction. I was given driving lessons and received my license without too much difficulty. However, I was an extremely anxious and cautious driver once the instructor no longer had control of the car. The problems worsened when I had to change lanes at high speed or in heavy traffic. I could not accurately judge the location of the other cars in relation to mine or the distance between my vehicle and others. Of course, I did not know that my perception was distorted. I was assured by everyone, "The problem is all in your head." In reality, my lack of confidence was a result and not the cause of my issues. I could not understand how my contemporaries could drive so confidently and enjoy being behind the wheel. The confusion I felt was similar to my experience years before, when my peers seemingly had no problem with stepping on the escalator. I desperately wanted the independence that driving offered, but it would require all of my courage and determination to turn that key! As had been true in previous cases, the "driving force" behind all this was pleasing my mother.

New York required high school students to pass statewide exams in several subjects in order to graduate. Students who scored well on the Regents examinations were awarded free tuition to state colleges. Awardees' names were posted on a bulletin board. It never occurred to me to check for my name. When a friend notified me that I was amongst those listed, I was genuinely shocked. I ran home to tell my mother the astounding news. She was putting away cans of tuna fish in our cupboard. I burst into the kitchen and blurted out what I could barely believe. She calmly continued stacking the tuna fish with little more than a word of congratulations. Mom was not given to displays of emotion, whether the situation was one of joy or sorrow. She and I often discussed her reaction (or seeming lack thereof) to that and other occasions. Given the formative nature of that particular experience, my mother and I began to describe her similar behaviors as "tunafishing."

Chapter 6

In my senior year of high school, a schoolmate introduced me to the man who would become my first husband. Steve had briefly dated a mutual friend and she was unavailable for a school dance, so he asked his friend's date if she could suggest someone else. I was very much attracted to the man I would marry. Steve was handsome, intelligent, considerate, of my faith, and he had a promising future. He was a student at a top engineering school, and intended to obtain his doctorate in chemical engineering. On one occasion, he invited me to view the room-sized computer at his school. It was extremely impressive, resembling the models used by mad scientists in movies. I very much enjoyed dating Steve. He was a member of a fraternity and we spent most weekends with his "brothers" and their girlfriends at the frat house, or joined other couples in low-cost activities. Steve found me very desirable, and expressed admiration for my character, intelligence and goals. His appreciation of these attributes was of great importance to me.

During our early dates, I recognized and valued some of the attributes that Steve shared with my father. I was unaware, however, of how much my future husband resembled my mother. After we had dated for about six months, I began to wonder if (or when) I would meet his parents. After picking me up, we often had occasion to drive through his parents' neighborhood. Each time Steve commented that we were near his home, my hopes were raised that he was planning to introduce me to his parents. Eventually, he did, and I found Trude and Max to be lovely people. At some point, I also met his younger siblings, Judy and Peter. Judy was a typical sixties teenager, and we easily became friends. I was surprised to find that Peter was very different from his older brother. Steve was modeling himself after his older cousin, "Big Freddie," who had lived upstairs from his family, with his parents, Freida and Mathias Austin. Big Freddie had earned a doctorate in engineering, an academic and career path Steve intended to emulate. Peter was very handsome and charming; girls were frequently calling him on the family phone. This amazed me as I believed that it was proper to wait for the male to initiate any interaction. Over time, I met the Kellys - Trude's sister Hilda, her husband, Karl, their two sons and their wives, "little" Freddie and his wife, Joanne, as well as Tony and his wife, Helene. Before coming to America, Hilda and Karl had changed their surname to protect themselves from the Nazis. Due to the family's harrowing experiences and few members, they lived close to each other and banded together. They enjoyed each other's company and the freedoms afforded by their new home. The families shared a beach cabana and I spent many happy weekends with them. We ate delicious picnic lunches with home-baked Viennese tarts for dessert. Given the scarcity of food for

Jews in occupied Austria, Trude was astonished that I only ate the open-faced sandwiches my mother prepared, in order to maintain an ideal weight.

At the time of our meeting, I had been accepted to Boston University, and my tuition was already paid. My parents insisted that I be enrolled there for my freshman year. My parents approved of Steve. However, mom strongly encouraged me to date others, stressing, "You must become more experienced." That piece of guidance was one of the very few that I disobeyed. I wouldn't risk the loss of that relationship. On my first free weekend, Steve drove up to give me his fraternity pin and I accepted. In my excitement, I had forgotten to sign in on my return to my dorm room, as was common policy at that time. Hours later the dorm mother shined a flashlight in my eyes, and warned me about expulsion. I was terrified about the consequences. However, this was not an unusual oversight for a freshman, and there were no repercussions. My mother, however, was furious about my pre-engagement. Distressed, I called my mother's best friend, Gertie, with whom I had a very close relationship. As in the past, she was able to effectively intercede.

Our relationship was fairly typical for a pre-engaged Jewish couple in the early sixties. Steve frequently visited me, renting a local hotel room. Part of the time was spent tutoring me in my areas of weakness. The rest of the weekend, we expressed our pent-up passion. Long-term goals and values enabled us to respect a boundary, thereby preventing pregnancy.

My first school break coincided with the Jewish High Holy Days. I asked my parents if I could observe them at home, as I had always celebrated the holidays with my family. However, my mother felt that as I had just arrived on campus, my prayers would be heard in Boston as well as in Brooklyn. Of course, my motivation for traveling home was not strictly religious, as I'm sure was apparent to my parents. Steve, however, convinced my mother that I should be allowed to come home: no small feat! I was tremendously impressed that he had been able to persuade her. I saw him as a latter-day Daniel, entering the lion's den, to emerge somewhat battered but victorious. I now had an ally who would champion my cause, and free me from the shackles of my mother's control. I prepared for my highly anticipated initial flight. What I did not anticipate during that short trip was that the severe motion sickness I endured as a child would reappear with a vengeance.

I experienced yet another unforeseen predicament during my trip home. I accompanied Steve and a group of his friends to the opening day of Shea Stadium. Although I am not a fan of baseball or any sport, I wanted to share in my future husband's activities. I hoped that, with time, I would start to enjoy watching baseball. This was my first experience in a stadium or any large structure of that sort. Shortly after being seated, I had to use the facilities. As I got up to go, Steve called after me, and asked if I had checked my seat number. Amazingly, I felt that I would be able to find him without that information. Of course, on returning, I had no idea where he was. I spent time going up and down each aisle, unaware that he and his friends were watching me, greatly amused. Angry with them and myself, I was determined to never let that reoccur. I began thinking about the many difficulties I had in directing others to my home; I even became confused within my own neighborhood. A pattern emerged. I decided to create a plan before leaving a location, to ensure a smooth return. I started with a simple and frequent scenario – leaving my seat in a restaurant that consisted of several rooms. I found some unique feature of the room, and committed it to memory to navigate my way back to my table.

Chapter 7

My freshman year at Boston University was an extremely stressful one for me, the city of Boston, and the entire country. It was the year that the Boston Strangler terrified our community and President Kennedy was assassinated. I found coursework to be much more difficult than anticipated. Therefore, I took a reduced course load every semester. This required me to enroll in summer sessions throughout my academic career. Unlike my friends, I did not engage in social activities. Studying took up all of my time. Freshman composition class was particularly frustrating. My comprehension of the material was good, as were my writing mechanics, but the instructor noted a significant problem in my organization of content. I could not grasp the principles of structure, and did not show any real progress. However, I passed and did well enough in my other classes to make the Dean's List. There was a ceremony for the parents of students so honored, and I was very happy and proud to see my mother and father in the audience.

I wanted to exceed my academic success as a freshman. That required me to build organizational structures for every area of my life. I had to externalize what I did not internally experience. When given a written assignment,

I attempted to develop a logical sequence for my thoughts, which resulted in many rough drafts. Once my work was completed, I critically reviewed it and made additional corrections. Unfortunately, my submissions were often returned with red marks all over the papers, as well as comments meant to be constructive. I also had to develop tools to manage time. I created daily, weekly and monthly calendars. These included every task and estimated the time each activity would require. This was particularly critical for long-term assignments. I divided all assignments, other than those due the following day, by the number of days until they were due. I then knew what I had to accomplish each day. These procedures enabled me to have the maximum time for rewrites. The repetition allowed me to compensate for a poor memory. Nevertheless, I was puzzled, frustrated and pained. "Why do I have to spend literally every waking hour on my studies? My classmates have time to enjoy sports, parties and gatherings with friends and family." However, for me and for students of my generation having similar challenges, these measures strengthened our creative capacities. Success was particularly sweet.

Upon completing my freshman year, I was determined to be admitted to Hunter College, part of the New York City University System. Admission was highly competitive, and a student could obtain an excellent education, virtually tuition-free. As Steve and I planned to marry at the completion of my sophomore year, I believed that the responsibility for college tuition should be ours. I was accepted and commuted to school by bus and subway, devoting myself to my studies and seeing Steve on the weekends. My parents had a small home in Brooklyn and my father had finished the basement, which housed a well-worn couch. This beloved piece of furniture held the bodily imprints, as well as sweet memories, of the three daughters and their prospective husbands. At curfew time, my dad would stand at the top of the stairs and whistle. On one occasion, he unexpectedly rushed downstairs, as there was a problem with the plumbing in the powder room. Fortunately, Steve kept cool, but moved quickly behind the boiler as we were not prepared to receive company!

By the time I completed my sophomore year, we had planned a lavish wedding and honeymoon. Several months before the event, I asked, "Uh... mom, how would you and daddy feel if I decided not to marry Steve now?"

"There is no problem with losing our deposits on the arrangements," Mom replied. "If you are unsure, tell us, and we will cancel everything." I dismissed any doubts as pre-wedding jitters. The wedding ceremony and reception exceeded all of our expectations. I was uncomfortable about being identified as a newlywed at a hotel, so we spent our first night as a married couple in our studio apartment. While avoiding discomfort, I soon encountered another, potentially life-altering circumstance. We were eager to become intimate with each other, but we were also inexperienced. The result was a mishap which could have resulted in pregnancy. Panicked, I followed the recommendation to prevent such an occurrence. I sat in the bathtub douching, a procedure that we now know could have resulted in conception. Needless to say, the evening was not the romantic interlude we had long anticipated. Our honeymoon was delayed several weeks so Steve could complete his semester. We flew to Puerto Rico and, after a few days, took a small plane to St. Thomas, and then a boat to St. John's. While I did not enjoy either St. Thomas or Puerto Rico, I was charmed by St. John's. We had a private bungalow with a waterfront view. Each day there was a beautiful luncheon buffet served in a lovely outdoor setting. Unfortunately, the trip home was far from idyllic. On returning to St. Thomas, I developed a gastrointestinal infection. This was significantly worsened by motion sickness during the returning air travels home. My in-laws picked us up at the airport. When my mother-in-law saw me, she exclaimed to Steve, "What did you do to her?"

With Steve's fellowships and the financial assistance of my parents, we were able to support ourselves. The plan was for me to graduate and provide for both of us until Steve earned his doctorate. Once he was established, I would have the opportunity to resume my schooling. Our studio apartment was near his school, and I commuted by subway to Hunter College. When not studying or visiting with family, we spent most of our leisure time with Steve's friends and their wives. Weekday evenings, I enjoyed the camaraderie of a group of wives, whose husbands were also enrolled in Brooklyn Polytechnic's doctoral program. On weekends, our group expanded to include his fraternity brothers from The Cooper Union and their spouses. When we needed an inexpensive treat, we drove to nearby Junior's to indulge in the world's best onion rings! Unfortunately, the good times we shared were not sufficient to sustain our union.

Our immaturity and lack of knowledge about my disorders were tremendous challenges. We were unprepared for the significant difficulties that lay ahead. These conditions, along with my childhood experiences, had discouraged me from developing a healthy sense of self, as a person separate from my mother. Although not fully conscious of this, I looked to my husband, who had many of my mother's attributes, to fulfill this role. When he did, I felt relieved, but also powerless and angry. Furthermore, when my mother and husband battled over certain issues, or the question of who would control me, it was excruciatingly painful.

My husband's relationship with his parents affected our marriage as well. While my in-laws were wonderful people, they were Holocaust survivors, and many of their family members were exterminated during World War II. As would be expected, this trauma, unimaginable to anyone who has not experienced it, would have a life-altering impact. Anything of significance that existed prior to their arrival in America (other than my father-in-law's breathtaking escape to freedom by skiing across the Alps) was not discussed. This avoidance of family history, and the void in communication which resembled my own, had a profound effect on Steve. Therefore, he brought his own poorly understood, unresolved conflicts into our marriage. We visited my in-laws every weekend. His father would watch sports on television. Steve would sit by his side, having little interest in sports. His mother would be at her sewing machine, supplementing the family income by dressmaking. The only voices that could be heard were mine and hers, as I was developing a relationship with my mother-in-law. On occasion, we would be treated to a wonderful Viennese menu of schnitzel (veal) and svetchkinroyster (fruit compote). I grew to love my in-laws. Max evidenced a cheery disposition, despite the trauma of fleeing for his life, while Trude was reserved. I had to earn her trust and affection, which I greatly prized. My in-laws enlisted me to negotiate with the Austrian embassy for reparations, and I was proud of my success in this very important undertaking. I knew a little of what life had been like before they emigrated to America. Nevertheless, I romanticized being in Vienna, before and after the occupation. I fantasized about wearing a beautiful gown, while Steve and I danced to Strauss waltzes, in an elegant ballroom.

Chapter 8

I was totally overwhelmed by my studies and household chores, as well as the social and emotional demands of a marriage. While Steve's program was very rigorous, he chose a field in which he was very strong. In addition, he had the experience and ability to manage the tasks associated with maintaining a household. Steve was not particularly disappointed by my lack of culinary expertise, as he was an excellent chef. He was very tolerant about all my difficulties with traditional wifely duties. However, Steve was far less agreeable about the hours I devoted to my studies. It seemed unreasonable that I had to spend at least twice the time that other accomplished students did to earn the same grades. I, too, had no explanation. Given my lack of experience and naivety, I had imagined that Steve would tutor me, as he had done when we were dating. And, in fact, there were instances when he did so. However, I did not anticipate how different our current circumstances would be from our expectations prior to our marriage.

It was very important for me to do as well in school as possible, for three reasons. The first was a practical matter. As I previously wrote, I believed it was my responsibility to pay for graduate tuition, and the City University was the only affordable option. Admission was highly competitive at that time, particularly for women. Second, I was dedicated to the idea of obtaining a doctoral degree in psychology, to uncover the sources of my difficulties, and to help others with this knowledge. Third, although it required enormous effort and sacrifice, I had attained success in academia, and was invested in continuing this achievement. Unfortunately, however, research did not exist to explain that my capacities to avoid distraction, concentrate, memorize, organize, sequence, spatially conceptualize, calculate efficiently, visually track across a page, accurately hear, exert fine motor control and write legibly, in conjunction with and exacerbating high levels of anxiety and depression, would take enormous amounts of dedication, time, and will to overcome. Steve was left with the impression that I was attempting to avoid him, and tensions between us escalated. However, I knew that academic success depended upon dedicating my efforts to my coursework. I was also devouring whatever research was available, in order to understand the cause of my difficulties. I fervently hoped that the information would lessen the tensions between us. I was living between the proverbial rock and a hard place!

Of course, the more time I spent seeking answers, preoccupied with painful issues, attempting to justify my seemingly paradoxical successes and failures, the greater the tensions became. As a psychology major, I was required to take statistics (or "sadistics" as I called it). After the midterm exam in the course, Dr. Stevens announced that everyone had failed, and our only grade would be the one earned on the final. Panicked, I hired a tutor, but the evening before the exam, my mind went completely blank. To his credit, Steve, who had not even taken a statistics course, taught me the entire subject overnight. This was particularly difficult. I had to have an in-depth understanding of the concepts because my memory for spatial/numerical material is so poor. We struggled mightily, but I earned an A in the course. I was very thankful for the help that Steve offered in my time of need. However, we generally were not very tolerant or supportive of each other's academic situations. I saw him as extremely intelligent, and as a student for whom studies came far more easily than they did for me. I could not understand the pressures and politics of obtaining a doctorate, no matter how bright a student might be, until I had the experience myself.

Chapter 9

During that time, I experienced my first incident of depersonalization. On what seemed an ordinary day, I looked in the mirror before going out and thought, "I wish I looked like that." Once I had that thought, I felt a profound fear, because it was irrational. I tried to intellectualize this phenomenon, but was unable to feel that the face in the mirror was mine. I began to struggle with the terrifying thought that this was a precursor to insanity. The early exposure to my cousin who was institutionalized had planted the seed of fear, which had been suppressed or repressed, and now began to assert itself. Due to several other powerful factors, I struggled to maintain a self-identity of any kind, to say nothing of a positive one. Unanswered questions about my parentage and undiagnosed symptoms of my disabilities undermined my development of a healthy, integrated sense of self. Then there was my overwhelming determination to do anything and everything to please both my mother and my husband. Unfortunately, they rarely agreed on what I should be doing. I no longer understood what I was feeling, or knew what I should be doing.

While I disappointed them in so many ways, there was one aspect of me in which both took great pride and pleasure - my appearance. Steve was very generous and enjoyed purchasing items to enhance my attractiveness. One very special evening, he surprised me with a shopping trip to the prestigious Bloomingdale's department store. Steve flagged down a taxi, a rare luxury, and we were "chauffeured" into Manhattan. I selected three beautiful outfits, and modeled each one for Steve, walking down an imaginary runway. I indeed felt like a model, as I returned, twirling with excitement. I was delighted to learn that he would be purchasing all three dresses! (I can still picture them today.)

Shopping for clothes with my mother was a very different experience than with my husband. I was always eager to shop with mom, as I had her undivided attention and dedication. Mom told me, "Marl, I can help you choose clothes that will maximize your assets and minimize your deficits." However, if I disagreed with her selections, or wore an item that she felt was unattractive, mom would say that I was either self-destructive or determined to punish her. She would call me before any event that we would be attending together, and ask what I would be wearing. An alternative would be suggested if my choice was unacceptable. While my appearance often garnered her praise, compliments provided at best a momentary pleasure. My public and acceptable persona was a creation of another person. Furthermore, as I previously wrote, being attractive felt threatening to me, after I was molested.

Interestingly, it was not the experience of depersonalization, the marital discord, or any of the other difficulties I've revealed that initiated my therapy. The incident that led to my psychoanalysis reveals a great deal about my relationship with my mother. Mom had been invited to my apartment for lunch, and found that the conditions were far from acceptable. "If you are on the honor roll," she said, "you can prepare good meals and maintain a clean, orderly and attractive home." She added, "As a wife, you should always be attractively dressed and wear makeup." Mom asked no more of me than she expected of herself. Her assumption about me was, of course, untrue. Poor fine motor coordination, spatial deficits, lack of experience and limited time, as well as painful memories, did not inspire me to improve my skills. After observation and reflection, mom determined that I would only subject her to my disordered apartment as a cry for help. An appointment was arranged with the relative of a friend who practiced psychoanalytically oriented therapy. Mom "sweetened the deal," by her promise of teaching me how to load my dishwasher in an organized way as an upcoming birthday gift!

As a Freudian-trained social worker, Rob interpreted many of my neurologically based deficits according to his theoretical framework. An essential goal of the therapy entailed my resolution of penis envy! While deeply confused about the nature of my difficulties, I explained to him that greater opportunities and not additional appendages were my objectives. Furthermore, Steve encouraged me to access his penis as often as possible!

In individual counseling, a therapist generally works one on one with a patient. Others are asked to participate only when input is required from a close relative(s) or from friend(s). Nevertheless, shortly after I began therapy, my mother wanted to enlist my therapist to support her in a conflict with my father. His father and stepmother lived near my parents, in a small apartment building. A half-sister and her family lived in the same building. My dad loved his family and was particularly attached to his father. His dad had conditions common to the elderly, with frequent doctor appointments. While dad's brother-in-law volunteered to provide transportation, my father insisted that he do the driving on every occasion, and his work schedule allowed for this. These errands took priority over any plans with my mother, which enraged her, despite her desire to develop a parental relationship with her in-laws. In addition, it caused sibling rivalry with his sister.

Chapter 10

While discussing these issues with Rob, my mother shared the actual circumstances of her relationship with my biological father. Over the course of my treatment, I was unable to compartmentalize the issues about my parentage. I told Rob that I questioned whether my father had indeed died serving in World War II. When I raised this issue, he encouraged me to discuss these doubts with my mother. When I did, she revealed the truth, and told me that she and my dad were completely supportive of my searching for my biological father. It was as if I had been emotionally holding my breath throughout my life, but exhaling was painful. Mom also told me that each time I vacationed in Kingston, she hoped that some family member would tell me the truth. That really surprised me. However, after giving it a great deal of thought, it occurred to me that she had been sending me mixed messages through the years. In addition, there had been no pictures of him nor of the two of them and mom never spoke of anything they had done together. There had never been even a trace of him, nor of any of his family. However, in my mother's words and tone of voice when speaking of Manny, I had inferred that my biological father was incapable of compassion and commitment, I admitted to myself the fear that mom would see me as having inherited my father's undesirable traits. I had been unable to provide a genuine and lasting reassurance for either of us that this was untrue. Therefore, I have had an excessive need to prove to myself and others that I was worthy of trust.

I can imagine how difficult it would have been for my mother to deal with her own feelings of abandonment, and to tell me that my father had chosen never to love, or even to know me. However, in virtually every other circumstance, she stated and acted upon her belief that a child should not be shielded from the realities of life. When would have been the time and the way to tell me the truth about my biological father? I do not know. I do, however, recall having a profoundly painful and frightening experience when the doubts I had suppressed for decades were brought to consciousness and confirmed. Shortly after I had "the discussion" with my mother, I was traveling by crowded subway to my college classes. As I looked around at the many men in my car, I had the thought that any one of them could be my father. This knowledge felt like an open, searing wound, as if I had been disassembled - I couldn't hold on to the fragments of myself. I was fearful that, like Humpty Dumpty, I could never be put back together again.

Although I graduated with honors, the job prospects for women with B.A. degrees, majoring in psychology, were limited. The first question I was asked was, "How fast can you type?" I could hunt and peck at best. Typing had been a required course in high school. However, I was unable to commit the keyboard to memory, and my poor eye-hand coordination caused me to continually strike the wrong key. My graduate application to the City University was rejected, and I was devastated. I had no significant support to cushion my rejection. None of my friends aspired to advanced degrees. Despite my academic achievements, my parents continued to assert that an undergraduate degree was sufficient to meet the status of helpmate. It could provide an income, should one be necessary at some future time. I was directed to find employment. This was not easily accomplished, as the male graduates were filling the entry-level administrative jobs. However bleak my prospects were, these were the sixties, and I was reading *The Feminine Mystique* and then *The Women's Room*. I knew I was not completely alone. I was strongly influenced and energized by the fledgling feminist movement. While my parents were concerned that they would see me on television as a radical bra burner, they needn't have worried. My physiology did not support that option! More importantly, my goals were equality in pay, opportunities to advance in employment and education, as well as to share household chores, and eventually child rearing.

I became increasingly desperate either to find employment in my chosen field or be accepted in a graduate program. Determined to support myself and Steve, I accepted a position as a research assistant in a Wall Street firm. Although this did not further my career goals, I found the study of economics fascinating, and believed this short-term venture would be very interesting. Unfortunately, this position was far from what I expected. Presumably, the firm had determined that hiring a female was in their best interest or met some requirement. I volunteered for any assignment for which I was equipped, only to find myself uncomfortably sitting at my desk with nothing to do. I knew the likelihood of acceptance to a doctoral program in psychology was remote. However, I was determined to be prepared should the opportunity present itself. In addition, I was bored to tears, and dreaded having nothing to occupy my mind for eight hours a day, five days a week. I decided to purchase books, enabling me to practice for the Graduate Record Exam and the Miller Analogy tests, required for admission to most graduate programs. Initially I was very concerned that my self-appointed "fellowship" would be detected. However, on no occasion did my colleagues even acknowledge my presence. My employment proved to be a good expenditure of time, as I did very well on both exams. Nevertheless, I had to resign when asked to clean the inside windows of my skyscraper office! As I was again unable to secure employment, my father was called upon to assist me. Initially, he pressured his broker to find an opportunity for me, to no avail. My mother then supported dad's desire to leave his position as a regional sales manager at Endo Pharmaceuticals, and work full-time in the stock market. His friend, who had seats on the American Stock Exchange, convinced my father to partner with him in establishing a firm to invest in unregistered stocks. This was a risky enterprise, as those stocks could not be sold until they were registered. My father arranged for me to be employed at his friend's firm, which was a family business. This proved to be disastrous. It was a high-pressure environment, for which I was totally unprepared. There was no time for instruction, and mistakes as well as hesitations were very costly. My hard-won academic achievements felt remote and inconsequential. Although my self-confidence had plummeted to a very low level, it was again time to move on.

Life on the home front was also a struggle. Steve was undergoing the emotional, educational and political difficulties endured by the majority of doctoral students. I would come home from work to find that he had been unable to accomplish anything for long periods of time. His anxieties and frustrations fueled mine in an unfortunate and probably all too common cycle. However, being intelligent and motivated, Steve persevered and found the resources he needed to achieve his goal. Somewhat surprisingly, one of those resources was my mother.

As I previously wrote, from the outset, they had a tempestuous relationship. Both attempted to control me, probably to allay their own anxieties. There were often conflicts which centered on me. Unfortunately, I did not have the personal strength to separate myself from either of them when the circumstances called for it. Nevertheless, when Steve was at a critical point in his doctoral program, he called upon my mother for advice. He was giving serious consideration to terminating his studies because of a difference of opinion with his advisor. My mother urged him to follow the course his advisor proposed and complete his dissertation. Should he choose, he could continue with the research, after attaining his degree. He followed her suggestion, and mom offered to type his dissertation, which she did without the benefit of a word processor! After gaining some skills and confidence, I found employment at another brokerage house, where the social atmosphere was more pleasant. The nature of the work was similar, but tolerable. It was a temporary measure because I intended to pursue my doctorate in the future.

Chapter 11

I became pregnant, as we had planned. My pregnancy was first suspected by my dentist. Apparently, the worsening of my periodontal condition heralded Erik's arrival. My dentist further noted that I had bony growths in front of and behind both upper and lower sets of teeth. This condition is defined as temporomandibular jaw, caused by the grinding of one's teeth. My dentist asked if I had been under significant stress. I had feared that it would be difficult for me to conceive, but we were successful on the first try! That accomplishment laid to rest concerns over my fertility. It was replaced by my anxieties over the wellbeing of our child and my ability to parent. The unspoken fear that began in my childhood, that I would face the same fate as my cousin, now expanded to include my child. Throughout my pregnancy, I was wracked with fear that my infant would be born with some type of abnormality, attributable either to some genetic defect or to a failure on my part. To alleviate the fear that my child might suffer the same fate, my mother revealed that Herbert's condition was not inheritable. However, the revelation fell far short of the intended impact, as I had lived with the unexpressed fear for over two decades.

I probably would have spent the entire nine months "wrapping myself in cotton balls." However, it was necessary for me to work up until about a month before my due date. I was commuting by subway to Wall Street. My morning sickness continued throughout my employment, and travel was particularly difficult. The commuters who had the dubious pleasure of accompanying me each day gave me a wide berth; I could be counted on to erupt as regularly as Old Faithful. Once in the office, my coworkers often had to yell questions to me, as I was frequently in the bathroom. Time was money and stock had to be processed, regardless of my condition. I maintained my position, despite my "delicate state," even during a recession, when many of my male cohorts were "downsized." I was even commended on my work ethic and attendance record. However, there was another reason I continued to be employed: a lecherous administrator, Dennis, whose hands roamed whenever he found an excuse to be next to me. This happened even during my pregnancy! Given my past, this made me sick with fear and anger, but I had to keep that job until Steve was assured of employment. I was prepared to leave at the first possible moment for a life supposedly destined to bring the rewards of financial and familial security, happiness and fulfillment.

About a month before my due date, Steve told me that he did not know whether he was ready to assume the responsibilities of parenthood. This was the first time he had said anything of the sort. With maturity and experience, I now understand that his feelings were completely normal. However, given my background, I was in a state of utter panic. I pleaded with him to talk to me about what he was feeling. In response, Steve said he could not discuss this with me. He would share his thoughts with Valerie, a female co-worker with whom we had become very friendly. This was not especially reassuring, but I saw no other option. Once again, I felt powerless, at a critical time in my life.

Steve called me at work with the wonderful news that he had successfully defended his dissertation. I was so thrilled and excited that I flung my arms in the air. The extensive, alphabetized pile of papers on the desk, which included every stock the firm was responsible for handling, fell to the floor. Ordinarily, I would have been terrified of losing my job and professed great remorse. However, I was so happy and relieved that I sat on the floor and calmly reached over my huge belly to pick up the papers surrounding me. I was in my ninth month and knew I would soon start my "real life" as a stay-at-home wife and mother.

Having earned his doctorate in Chemical Engineering, Steve was hired by Exxon. We had to move to a garden apartment in West Orange, New Jersey. Although I looked forward to becoming a full-time homemaker and mother, I was anxious about my abilities to be the best possible wife and parent. Nothing else in my life took on the importance of giving our child everything he required to have a healthy, safe, happy and secure childhood. As is true for most parents, I was determined to learn what to do and not to do, based on my childhood experiences and upbringing. I continued with my therapy. Steve drove me to my weekly appointment in Manhattan, where he had his own appointments. My parents were very generous, and in a position to give us financial assistance. We used their gifts to buy items needed or wanted by young couples starting their lives together. We were able to purchase beautiful furnishings, which I very much appreciated and enjoyed shopping for with my mother.

Chapter 12

My water broke at noon one clear day in February. My mother, who was visiting, was enlisted to drive me to the hospital. My labor was lengthy, and I was wracked with pain and fear about complications. After many hours, I waddled out to the waiting room and "requested" that my husband be with me. Steve did sit by my bedside and read magazines, while I experienced what the shouting in adjoining labor rooms was all about. I now understand it was not lack of concern, but a feeling of powerlessness, which prompted his behavior. At a time of great and myriad emotions for us both, I felt no comfort and support, but seemed alone at this monumental undertaking in my life. My obstetrician, Dr. Gregori, appeared concerned and performed various tests. Ultimately, she said that a caesarian would be necessary, as my son could not be delivered through the birth canal. The fears about my child's well-being that I had throughout my pregnancy, together with the pain, were almost unendurable. However, once he was born, I experienced the indescribable joy of this miracle. Having been spared a trip down a very tight and viscous passage, he emerged looking beautiful and healthy. I unwrapped his blanket and checked to see that he came with all equipment intact. Now it would be my responsibility to protect and nurture this precious gift.

Following our Jewish tradition, we named our son after deceased relatives. His first name would honor my beloved Aunt Etta, and his middle name honored Steve's grandfather, David. As I needed a name beginning with "E", there were a number of choices, and I didn't want the selection to be completely random. Once engaged in the process, I recalled a very happy childhood memory. Caroline Neilson, of Norwegian heritage, was one of my early schoolmates, and a good friend. Each afternoon, when we were dismissed for lunch, we walked to her nearby home. Her warmhearted mother treated us to rice and milk soup. What made this luncheon even more special were Caroline's two handsome teenage brothers. At that time, I was also influenced by a commercial, which featured a striking man, who was sailing a Viking ship. The advertised cigarette product was called "Erik." While I did not expect my son to resemble a Viking, I felt good about the association. So we named our son Erik David.

In 1971, a woman who had a cesarean was in the hospital considerably longer than would be the case today. As I prepared to go home, I asked my husband to bring a dress that I had worn prior to my pregnancy. Feeling svelte, I was eager to put my maternity clothes in storage. It was time to resume wearing my more fashionable and form-fitting outfits. Much to my surprise and unhappiness, I had to wear a housecoat home, as I could not fit into anything I had previously worn. I now had to purchase some new garments, and pay the price for all those goodies I had eaten, with abandon, over the past nine months. It would be many years before I lost the weight I had gained in my pregnancy.

Steve had picked up the nurse who was recommended by our friends, and Erik and I were driven home. Once there, I prepared for my family's arrival, in a few days, for Erik's Bris (circumcision). Unfortunately, a severe winter storm was forecast for the day of the event. I was panicked, and did not want my parents and elderly relatives to risk driving from Brooklyn to West Orange in bad weather. However, my family would not consider missing this religious celebration. While their travel went smoothly, other disturbances arose. We had engaged a rabbi to perform the circumcision. Our nurse expressed concern that the table Erik would be on was not sufficiently sturdy, but the rabbi disagreed. An argument ensued, and it was a while before they reached a compromise. At that point, I was told to go into another room, until the procedure was completed. I did so, but could still hear Erik cry out once. I then began to cry myself (and, as is true with most parents, it would be the first of many times that I would cry when my child did.)

I loved the earliest stages of his infancy, and marveled over each of Erik's accomplishments. He was a beautiful, inquisitive, very active and happy baby. However, once he was able to walk, the concerns about his well-being, which I felt throughout my pregnancy, escalated. I virtually never let down my guard while he was awake. Of course, it was not possible to prevent all illnesses and accidents. There were two incidents of significant concern in Erik's early childhood. When he was about five months old, severe diarrhea began and continued to worsen, despite all the interventions of his pediatrician. We were told that a diagnostic test had to be administered, as soon as possible, and the procedure itself was very risky. Although I was ambivalent about my faith, in desperation, I prayed to my Aunt Etta to intercede. The next morning, the day of the assessment, the diarrhea had completely ceased and never returned. The physicians had no explanation. I leave it to you, the reader, to reach your own conclusion.

The second incident occurred when Erik was a toddler. My parents had converted a large closet in our apartment into a changing room. We had taken off the door, but neglected to remove the hinges. I was standing in front of the room, at arm's length from him. Erik tripped and his chin was deeply cut by the bottom hinges. Blood began to spurt out. My initial response was hysteria, but a mothering instinct calmed me. Although I had my license, I was reluctant to drive, particularly with Erik in the car. Not knowing any neighbors, I quickly phoned the police. They promptly responded, and drove us to Erik's pediatrician, Dr. Maron. I held back my tears as the doctor stitched Erik's chin. As always has been the case, my son bravely endured the procedure.

I had felt that Erik was only safe when he was with me (and even then I could not always reassure myself), or with my parents. Perhaps due to my anxiety, I had foresight regarding issues of child safety. Prescient, I saw the need for child auto seats, bicycle helmets, cabinet locks, softer surfaces for playgrounds, and so forth. I could not understand why other parents and caregivers seemed so relaxed as their charges faced one danger after another. When invited to a neighbor's house, I was torn between having a conversation and keeping a constant eye on my son. I did not want to seem unnaturally preoccupied, nor spoil his fun. I was tormented, and lost complete confidence in my ability to make judgments concerning Erik's physical well-being. When his father and I went visiting, as was generally common at the time, childcare was solely my responsibility. I became totally exhausted, both physically and mentally.

My mother was concerned about anxiety and stress causing my health to suffer. This would then impact everyone in the family. She began to think about how she could offer a means of easing particularly onerous tasks. Ultimately, she focused her attention on my laundry responsibilities. The washers and dryers in our apartment complex were in the basement of a building, on the other side of a central square lawn. As Erik was an infant, I had to bundle him up in clothing, socks, shoes, a snowsuit and a hat. I then had to pack diapers, a change of clothes, bottles, snacks, toys, and a pacifier in a bag. Another bag filled with laundry products had to be packed for our little journey. I would then carry him and all the paraphernalia across the green, and navigate the stairs. Of course, a diaper deposit often necessitated undressing and redressing all layers that I had just put on. My mother came up with a plan to greatly simplify this task. She researched a small portable washing machine that could be hooked up to the bathroom sink. Clothes would then be placed on a unit in the tub to dry. I could do laundry at my convenience, and complete other chores or relax while Erik was napping or in a playpen. I was thrilled about receiving this gift! However, my joy was short-lived.

Steve was opposed to my parents funding this. He felt that we should wait until he could afford to purchase the machine. I understood that, as the breadwinner, Steve believed that accepting the machine would be damaging to his pride. In addition, he saw this offer as an example of mom controlling our lives, and was therefore extremely resistant. I had to decide, and after much angst, chose the freedom the washer offered me. I relished the ease the machine provided. However, I regretted that Steve and I could not work through this issue.

My husband and I visited his parents almost every weekend. While my in-laws were loving grandparents, they did not feel it necessary to do any childproofing or close observation of my son. In response to my concerns, they attempted to assure me that my child had a level of understanding that was not possible. Yet, I doubted myself. The situation was brought to a head when my in-laws offered to watch Erik, so that Steve and I could vacation. They neglected to put him in the car seat we had left, and chose to have him sit on my mother-in-law's lap. While he was uninjured, I obsessed over what might have happened, and was distrustful and angry. I resumed therapy to deal with these feelings, but it was no help. I was becoming frightened and discouraged over finding an appropriate psychologist. I eventually decided to be seen by a psychiatrist, who could treat me with pharmaceuticals. When all the antianxiety and antidepressant drugs failed to bring about a sufficient reduction in my symptoms, I was given benzodiazepines. Less was understood then about the highly addictive danger of certain classes of drugs than is known today. Finally, I felt relief, and could fulfill my responsibilities as Erik's mother. I understood that Xanax, Lorazepam and other benzos had to be taken only as prescribed, and with awareness of any potentially dangerous side effects upon use. I believed that if I followed the directions, I would be safe.

It was clear to me that Erik had to interact with other children, without my interference. There were no children in our apartment complex or in the immediate neighborhood. I found a cooperative play school that required limited involvement on my part. On Erik's first day, the director told me to wait in a different room from the one my son was in, and observe his reaction to my absence. After a short while, I peeked in to see him happily at play, and left to return two hours later. Not only was he fine without his mommy, he had a rare meltdown when it was time to leave. I was concerned that the staff would think that I was abusing him at home! Erik attended one day a week and continued to very much enjoy himself without his hovering mother. As a "staff member", I had the reassurance of seeing that the children were well attended.

There was, however, one major problem – transportation. I had to drive him to school. We lived in a small town and the school was nearby. However, I experienced a tremendous dread each time driving was required. I faced a terrible conflict. As with many other seemingly ordinary tasks, I tormented myself. How did the other mothers appear to handle this task with ease? When any driving was coupled with looking for a new location, the tension was almost unbearable. My family and friends continued to assure me, "It is all in your head." Nevertheless, prior to an appointment, my parents drove me to a destination, and pointed out markers along the way. This unofficial "accommodation" was extremely helpful.

Despite the need for this assistance, my mother attributed my profound fear of driving, from my quiet suburb to her heavily trafficked area, to malevolence. This interpretation was similar to the reason she gave for me stepping on her shoes, many years ago. Mom now attributed my reluctance to a wish to avoid being with her. Of course, by that time, it was a self-fulfilling prophecy. Nevertheless, I blasted Mozart, sweated profusely and prayed that I would live to complete the journey, as huge trucks tailgated my tiny, slow-moving Honda on the New Jersey Turnpike.

Chapter 13

Once my son established some friendships, and my husband was engrossed in his work, I began to think of pursuing my doctoral studies. Unfortunately, this ultimately proved to be the end of our marriage. After dinner, my husband would sit in front of our television to complete work. I wasn't able to question him to any great degree about his occupation as it was highly technical. My understanding of what he did was very limited. However, Steve felt that it was my duty to remain in our family room with him, even if I did not care to watch the chosen television show. I was bored, and found this level of control intolerable. In addition to providing intellectual stimulation, there were several reasons that school continued to exert a strong emotional pull. I continued to believe that, through my studies, I would learn why I tortured myself, and what I could do to become healthier. I also worried that Steve would grow bored of a wife that had not developed herself. Most importantly, I feared becoming emotionally over-invested in Erik, without another meaningful activity.

With great trepidation, I applied to a Master's program in Clinical Psychology and was accepted at a local university. I began my course work in the evening, taking one course at a time. Of course, driving, particularly at night, presented an enormous problem. Steve and I had maintained a close relationship with his colleague. Valerie had separated from her husband and lived in an adjoining town. Once my classes started, Steve decided that it was unsafe for Valerie to travel unaccompanied to her apartment, which was located in a nearby suburban town. He arranged to follow her home, where she would park her car and be driven to our house to keep him company. Meanwhile, I drove to a large campus and walked alone on it. On my return, he would drive Valerie home. I asked Steve why he was unconcerned about my safety. He replied, "This is necessary because of your anxieties." I never questioned him again about this.

Despite the overwhelming pain and fear this caused, I desperately wanted Erik to grow up in a home with two loving parents. I wrestled with the idea of abandoning my plans of returning to school, but that course also seemed to lead to disaster. Education was my only hope of dealing with the confusion and torment which prevented me from becoming the wife and mother, the person I so desperately wanted to be. Our mutual "friend," Valerie, told me, "Your desire to go to school is pure selfishness." I had not developed any other close relationships after moving into our house. My parents did not understand my drive, but they were supportive, as attending graduate school was important to me. Nevertheless, they were not in a position to provide transportation. Terrified to get behind the wheel on dark, winding roads, treacherous in inclement weather, I prayed for my safety. My goal was to do “what is right for Erik and me.” Walking alone on the campus, I tried to block the vision of my husband and “best” friend discussing my deficiencies, and enjoying each other’s company. I did not allow myself to think about what the implications were for the development of a physically intimate relationship between them. At least on a conscious level, I did not and do not believe that my husband would betray my trust in that manner. Nevertheless, the pain was almost unendurable. His refusal to transport (and therefore support and protect) me has had many profound ramifications. Not only was my anxiety exacerbated, I feared that revealing it to others would again lead to my abandonment or another “punishment.” This fear was then generalized to many other situations.

My anxiety, indecision and lack of confidence became more pervasive as I tried to be a good mother, wife, daughter and student. I hoped that education, therapy and dedicated introspection would result in my more normal functioning. Eventually, my family, my sanity and my physical well-being might be preserved. However, time was running out. I would come home from class excited about what had been discussed. Steve was not open to a conversation about what I was learning. In contrast, we discussed his office’s politics and personalities. Steve was an early feminist. He was keenly aware that his female colleagues did not have the opportunities that their skills warranted. He was genuinely outraged by this, and used whatever means at his command to champion their respective causes. Unfortunately, being his wife meant I didn’t benefit from this progressive perspective.

We wanted to reach out to each other. For many reasons, however, we were unable to do so, and became progressively more alienated from each other. Under terrific stress, I was hospitalized with pneumonia. My very high fever required me to be packed in ice, and I began to hallucinate. As I am allergic to the drug of choice, penicillin, there ensued a prolonged period of trials until an effective antibiotic was found. As I regained rationality, I had one overriding thought: a determination to recover, so that Erik would have two loving parents. Steve was devoted to him, and less unreasonably fearful. However, I believed that my involvement in raising Erik provided an important balance.

Once my lungs were clear, I was released from the hospital. A low-grade temperature developed that sapped my strength and I was diagnosed with a severe sinus infection. I suffered from debilitating fatigue, which left me unable even to dress myself. I was panicked, as the condition was resistant to all treatment. My son was very young during that period. My mother assisted me in caring for him, because I was sleeping for most of the day. I was agonizingly conflicted over whether to continue with my marriage. Given my early deprivation of a father, and the subsequent experience of how critically important a relationship it was, I had vowed never to be the cause of that devastating loss for any child of mine. However, my health was in serious jeopardy. Then too, I questioned whether it was better for Erik to be raised in a marriage lacking support, communication and genuine intimacy. On reflection, what I attributed to the death of love was great anger and a sense of betrayal. However, my self-esteem and confidence were shattered. I had tremendous doubts about how well I could care for my son as a single parent. Should we separate, I could not decide whether Steve or I could provide the emotionally healthier and safer environment.

During one of her many weekly visits, my mother pronounced, "You are suffering from the 'blue bathrobe syndrome'," as I had enough energy to put only that on. (She and I believed ourselves qualified to make submissions to the Diagnosis and Statistical Manual of the American Psychological Association. Our first submission was "tunafishing," as I explained earlier. Mom diagnosed me as "emotionally paralyzed by deciding whether to continue your marriage." I reflected on this, and concluded that without consciously determining to do so, I had used this recovery period to decide that my marriage should end. Steve pleaded with me to reconsider, promising, "Changes could be made in our relationship." I gave it a great deal of thought, but did not understand all of the feelings that were underlying this decision. I believed that it would be immoral for me to live with Steve, and continue my education, when there was no possibility of reviving my love for him. Later, I asked Steve to consider reconciliation. By then, he had met the woman who was to become his wife. I was sad, but of course completely understood. Due to my feelings of guilt and failure, I refused to accept what Steve offered me as we divided our belongings. I even dismissed the experienced lawyer who was advising me about what I was entitled to under the law. Instead, I chose a family member who had just passed the bar, telling him, "I want only child care and alimony until I find employment." I agreed not to take any of Steve's pension, in exchange for guaranteeing that Erik would receive everything he required. I should have known that Steve would have done so anyway.

Chapter 14

Erik was about four when his father and I separated. It was the beginning of an incredibly challenging yet productive era for me. Erik and I moved into a one-bedroom garden apartment complex, and Steve rented a one-bedroom apartment in an adjoining town. I felt that it was critically important for Erik to have his own room. Therefore, I purchased a sleeper sofa to be in the living room for me. As a young child, my son suffered from chronic ear infections, and associated respiratory ailments. For years, Erik would awake in the night, screaming in pain, with a burning fever. I would rush him to the emergency room, where he would be administered a codeine-based medication and antibiotic. Once treatment was completed, he developed another infection. Due to the serious nature of his condition, I relied on my mother to care for him while I attended school. Although I knew that he was in good hands, it was very difficult and painful for me to leave when he was ill. In addition to my love and concern, I experienced guilt about not fulfilling my duties as a mother. I also felt guilty about my mother, who sacrificed attending the college course in which she had just enrolled, and very much enjoyed. I told myself, "If I had followed her advice, I would have spared her, my father, my child and Steve from suffering."

I expressed my regrets and asked my parents how I could repay their devotion. They replied, "Pass it on." My mother said, "You are destined to draw upon your experiences and strategies, to support students who are considered bright, but have inexplicable learning challenges." When tired and discouraged, I imagined myself holding on to students who were clinging to a cliff, over a precipitous drop. All my suffering and that of my family members had meaning, if I were to move forward.

Nevertheless, as I prepared to leave for class, Erik's illness, doubts about my capabilities, and driving difficulties intensified my chronically high level of anxiety. My abilities to attend, concentrate and function academically were further impeded. I was continually operating at an almost unbearable level of stress. While encouraged to continue my studies, I was paralyzed with indecision about whether to surgically treat Erik's chronic ear infections. My mother again offered support, and we decided to have myringotomy tubes placed in his ears. The operation was successful, and my son regained his health.

Given how conflicted I felt about myself and my life, I was astounded that several women I knew, who appeared to be happily married and financially secure, told me that they were envious of my sense of purpose. Others described me as driven or, conversely, a perennial student, and I was unable to view myself in a positive light.

As I advanced in my schooling, aspects of the work were increasingly challenging and absorbed virtually all of my time. I was required to recruit twenty-five adults, to whom I would administer a complete psychological battery. As would be expected, very few people I approached were eager to take an I.Q. test and personality assessments. My parents graciously accepted, and did well. Steve also volunteered, saying that he would do anything to hasten my graduation. I jokingly quipped that I should have conducted the exams before marriage, and would do so in the course of future dating! Statistics continued to be a struggle, as it was for most psychology majors. More troublesome however were significant problems I had in administering tests and writing reports about the results of the testing. The Wechsler battery that I was trained to administer required me to have good eye-hand coordination and spatial memory, both significant areas of deficit. With a great deal of practice, I was able to adequately perform these tasks. However, I continued to have considerable challenges in report writing, despite repetition and feedback. These reports required a very high level of organization. I had to integrate findings from a number of different tests, and experienced overwhelming difficulty in overcoming the executive limitations that had plagued me since elementary school. One of my professors would show me another student's report, and instruct me to use it as a model. He would say, "As my most promising student, you should see what is needed and produce it." The comparison enabled me to see that my report was poorly structured. However, I struggled to use the model as a guide, despite making an inordinate effort. I was puzzled and frustrated, as were my professors. Each one would say something like, "You have an excellent understanding of the theoretical concepts, establish a good rapport with clients, and demonstrate insights about diagnosis and treatment. Why can't you organize your material?" The stress took its toll on my health, and I had to withdraw for the semester.. Once more, I was faced with an agonizing dilemma. I couldn't think of another area of study where I would be as emotionally invested, and more likely to succeed. Learning disabilities were just beginning to be recognized as a syndrome in the early seventies. One narrow conceptualization described a learning disability as a reading disorder that was experienced in childhood. I had been an excellent reader into my adulthood. Therefore, it didn't occur to me that my poor spatial capacities and miscalculations were indications of several learning disabilities. As for my disorganization, attentional deficits and executive dysfunctioning - these too were not yet conceived of as manifestations of disorders.

I learned that sacrificing virtually every activity, other than study and parenting, resulted in academic success in my M.A. program. Having earned an almost-perfect GPA and being well prepared, I anticipated doing very well on my comprehensive exams. Opening the envelope with the test results, I was shocked and shattered to read that I had failed both portions of the test. This required me to "sit out" a year before retaking the exam. If unsuccessful on the second attempt, I would forfeit my degree. Stunned, and hoping that a grading mistake had been made, I called my advisor. Dr. Davis told me, "I and the entire faculty in the graduate department of psychology are astounded by your failure. We are literally at a loss for words. None of us felt prepared to share this information with you." My initial reactions to hearing these devastating words were shock and anger. I could not believe or accept that my professors, who were extremely articulate and well trained, were unable to reach out to me at this time. Still questioning their judgment, I asked for and received a copy of my test. I then made an appointment with a psychologist who was a family friend. She reviewed my responses and confirmed that my essays were not of passing quality. I was then referred to a school psychologist for tutoring in report writing. I could no longer deny the reality of my deficits, nor the circumstances I was facing. However, I still had no answer as to why I was unable to attain goals that seemed reasonable, based upon my apparent abilities and achievements (although admittedly they were puzzlingly inconsistent.) This was true, despite the searing self-analysis I continued to conduct for as long as I could remember.

I was distraught over having to communicate my failure to my parents and son. I could not even soften the blow in a meaningful way, as I also had been unable to secure employment. I would, therefore, have to ask my former husband for an extension of financial support, a painful and humiliating prospect. My health, finances, and my relationships with friends and family had progressively deteriorated, increasing my sense of isolation. Even more devastating was my limited self-understanding and diminished ability to control my emotions. Chronic but minor conditions worsened, and I was not expected to survive a second bout of pneumonia. My therapist at the time had warned, "These illnesses are attempts to escape from circumstances that have become overwhelmingly painful and exhausted almost all of your resources." Despite questioning whether it would not be an act of love to spare my parents and child from having their hopes continually dashed, to spare myself from being the unwilling and unwitting source of their great pain, unable to understand the inconsistencies and difficulties or how to proceed, somehow I went on.

Desperately seeking answers and a resolution, I made two appointments. The first was with a psychiatrist, who sought to uncover the biological basis for my difficulties and to treat them with medication. My mother wrote the following passage in response to the doctor's request for information about her pregnancy and the days after my birth.

"In the Beginning there was Marlene, Me and G-d.

Two major occurrences profoundly impacted my life in August 1945. One was the cataclysmic event that ended World War II. The other was the birth of my baby daughter, Marlene. I hazily remember the doctor telling me that I had a beautiful baby girl. Silently, I gave thanks to G-d because she was healthy." (In my adulthood, my mother confided that her initial reaction was that I was ugly. This was a tremendous disappointment as she had understandable pride in her striking appearance and her perception deepened the pain and fear she felt in our circumstance.) "While I was hospitalized, all radio programs were interrupted by special bulletins announcing that a bomb had been dropped on Hiroshima, Japan. It was a hot, humid period and through the open windows came the sound of the overwhelmingly joyous response to the news that the War was coming to an end. People were laughing and crying, bells were ringing, horns were blowing, and hysteria reigned.

In the midst of all of this pandemonium I quietly lay on my hospital bed, reflecting on what the future would hold for us. World War II was considered to be the war to end all wars. Ironically, however, our struggle for survival was just beginning and loomed as a frightening specter. When entering the hospital, I knew that I would be bringing Marlene up as a single parent. My husband had been previously married and fathered children from that union. During my pregnancy, he told me that he was unable to meet the demands of our marriage and what would be his fourth child. He would provide financial support, but felt it best to have no contact, direct or indirect, with the child.

The day I brought Marlene home from the hospital is seared in my memory. I entered the empty apartment, holding my child. Locking the door, I sat down on a chair with this five-day-old infant for whom I was totally responsible and began to cry. Our future looked very bleak. The youngest of eight siblings, only my youngest brother and I were first generation Americans. My childhood was marked by extreme poverty. As we could afford only the barest minimum of medical care, I nursed my mother through her agonizing struggle with cancer. She succumbed to it when I was 17 years old and my father died a few years later. In the midst of the Great Depression, I was employed as a secretary in an insurance office, and of necessity, became financially independent. I was also called upon to assist my sisters with their children, and became very attached to my sister Etta. We were much alike in nature, but separated by a generation and I looked upon her as a mother. We had become estranged, as she was vehemently opposed to my marriage. In response to my pregnancy, she suggested that I allow Marlene to be adopted by a couple in our family unable to have children and have her raised as their own. Despite my great emotional pain and fear, having a child was an intensely powerful driving force within me for as long as I could remember. I knew it would be impossible for me to see another couple parent my child. My early background precluded me from indulging in the luxury of self-pity. Slowly, I dried my tears, hugged my baby and said, 'Marlene, it is you and I against the world, but somehow we will make it'. At the time of my marriage, I had moved from a small town in upstate New York into an apartment in Brooklyn, New York City, and it took seven months before it was possible for me to get a telephone installed. Not only was I alone with my baby, without a phone I was totally cut off from voice communication with anyone who could have provided comfort and support. So started our Odyssey."

Unfortunately, the medication prescribed by the psychiatrist was not helpful. However, my mother's writing provided me with nuanced material that deepened my understanding of her and possibly of myself. My reaction to her memoir evoked deeply felt emotions and images. Perhaps, as research has suggested, her state of mind regarding our circumstances was communicated to me while in utero, and her distress grew within me.

The second appointment I made was with the school psychologist I had been referred to for tutoring. She resided in a town adjacent to the city where my parents lived. My mother met me after my appointments to provide support and treat me to dinner. She said that when I came out of Dr. Rubins's office, my face was so red she feared I was having some sort of attack. In addition to the stress of the appointment, traveling to the psychologist's office meant driving on fast-moving, heavily congested highways. I had to navigate my small car away from tractor trailers, whose tailgating came close to paralyzing me with fear. However, it appeared to be my only alternative to achieving a passing grade and employment. For a year, I made what was for me a perilous weekly trip. With a great deal of work, it improved my ability to organize my thoughts and data in writing.

On the day I was to retake my "comps," I was literally sick with fear. However, I managed to sit for the entire exam and apply my tutor's schema. My mother happened to be visiting me on the day the envelope with testing results was delivered. I was emotionally frozen, unable to open it. At day's end, when she was about to leave, mom said, "I insist that you open that envelope. I will not leave until you do." When I seemed unable to move, she took it from my hand and, slowly, opened it. I literally could not breathe and time stood still. Gradually, a look of relief and then joy emerged from her tightly composed expression. Deliberately, she said, "You passed." I had been given a reprieve, but my happiness and encouragement about the future was short-lived.

Still unable to secure a job in the field of psychology, I applied for a number of positions, for which I had no training, skill, or interest. On one occasion, I answered an ad for a customer service representative in a bank. I went to the interview with trepidation. Any position that involved numbers was certain to be difficult. However, I was under the impression that interacting with clients and describing the bank's services would be the bulk of my work. I was also desperate for income, and the bank was located only about one block from my apartment. This enabled me to greet my son when he came home from school. Unfortunately, the job entailed sitting in front of a computer screen, composed entirely of numbers, while I tried to calm irate customers and research their accounts. Soon after I started, the supervisor called me into her office and said, "Despite your efforts, you aren't suited for the job." She was, of course, correct. Steve suggested that I apply to McDonalds for whatever position was open. This devastated me. It appeared that the many years I dedicated to my studies, the financial and personal costs, as well as the sacrifices that I and my family made were in vain. Even worse, I didn't believe that I could clean or prepare food adequately enough to maintain my employment in a fast food establishment!

After exhausting every option that was available, I needed to get additional, short-term, low-cost training. At that time, the computer industry was starting to thrive. Knowing full well that my abilities lay elsewhere, I nonetheless felt that there was little choice but to seek some affordable instruction in computing. I took an aptitude test at Chubb Institute, but was not accepted into their program. Undaunted, I enrolled in a computer course at a local community college. There, it was confirmed that I am not a detail-oriented person, nor is my strength in the requisite logic underlying programming. I could not even enter data quickly and accurately enough for that type of position.

Chapter 15

I was searching for answers to my employment dilemma, and to understand why my very bright son was experiencing difficulties in school. Of course, I knew that he was greatly impacted by his parents' divorce. However, I considered the possibility that Erik might also have a problem with learning. While I was researching that possibility, Steve's wife, Carolyn, returned from a California business trip with a newspaper article that changed our lives. Written by Kathy Rich, in the October 28, 1981 edition of the San Francisco Chronicle, it was entitled, "A Handicap That Makes Geniuses Look Like Idiots." Rich wrote that if she hadn't read Eileen Simpson's *Reversals: A Personal Account of Victory Over Dyslexia*, she "would have gone on believing that I was lazy or absentminded. Reading her autobiography was like a religious experience for me. Here, finally was someone who knew, someone who gave me an explanation for all my backward behavior." She went on to provide information about the condition, well-known Americans who presumably suffered from it, its manifestations, and treatments. Rich went on, "Most dyslexics' lives have been scarred with continual reminders of 'how stupid' they are...Most dyslexics I know are constantly on guard against sabotaging themselves at the office... The key to coping with dyslexia is to work with, rather than resist, the debits... Through understanding and patience, my handicaps no longer crush, but merely annoy me."

Upon reading the article that my former husband had brought to me, I was astonished. The article shed no light on Erik's academic issues. His subsequent evaluation found him to be gifted, with no evidence of a learning disability. However, lifelong difficulties of mine were clearly enumerated and described as learning disabilities. Dr. Levinson, a physician mentioned in the article, discovered that a great number of adult dyslexics had phobias involving space and motion - fears of heights, driving, walking down stairs, and so on. He concluded that dyslexia was somehow linked to a disorder of the inner ear system, the network responsible for balance and coordination. Although it was not clear why antihistamines reduced the level of dyslexic disorders and attendant phobias, half of his patients improved with medication.

With astonishment, trembling and through tears, I read and re-read the article. I finally had an answer to my question, "WHAT IS WRONG WITH ME?" As I previously wrote, I had difficulty with most of the behaviors he identified. This article would radically impact the course of my life. After taking some time to absorb the information, I made an appointment with Dr. Levinson. His approach, which was "somewhat more controversial, aimed at alleviating, rather than unraveling, the disorder by prescribing a combination of carefully selected antihistamines." The appointment was a very difficult one, in that I experienced a number of significant deficits, of which I was previously unaware. I was first asked to remove my shoes, close my eyes and walk a straight line. Having never done this before, I assumed that this simple task could be easily accomplished. However, my frustration and embarrassment grew as I found myself unable to do it. An EEG test measured my ability to track and focus my eyes. Again, significant deficiencies were noted. The last test seemed innocuous enough in its description. However, anyone who has taken this test will appreciate how truly horrific it can be. A few drops of warm and then cold water were placed in alternate ears through a small pipette. I felt that my head was going to explode. After the worst had passed, I lay on the table, dizzy and nauseated for what seemed like endless hours. Apparently, that test diagnosed significant vestibular (balance) dysfunction. The evaluators stated, "You must be a genius to have accomplished what you did, while contending with the neurological impairments that we found." I certainly did not see myself as a genius! While that testing was useful, additional information was needed. The neurologist referred me to a neuropsychologist, where I was given a comprehensive battery. It indicated that I had superior verbal abilities, and was significantly weaker in my non-verbal problem-solving capabilities. I had even done poorly on a section of the test that, as a student, I had administered. Limitations were also found in my attentional abilities, but there was little specific assessment for ADHD at that time.

This information impacted my self-image, just as absorbing the facts of my parentage had, so many years ago. Those of us with "invisible disabilities" cannot be meaningfully protected from dealing with the reality of our conditions, any more than from the other fundamental aspects of our lives. Without this knowledge, we are limited in our understanding of who we are and what we need to grow. Current research underscores the extraordinary will and effort required to finally accept a difficult truth about oneself and move forward. Assimilating this information into one's sense of self and reality, which has been artfully constructed and defended over time, extracts a significant cost in pain.

In an unfortunate coincidence, I received the neuropsychological report on the day that a newsletter was sent to the alumni of my graduate program. It listed the accomplishments of my fellow students. Many of them were enrolled in doctoral programs or had progressed in their careers. I was devastated and frightened by my initial thoughts - that I would never be able to complete my studies and become a psychologist. Struggling with overwhelming emotions, I attempted to calm myself as I had many times over the years, and create a direction forward. There would be a path for me but, most likely, a steeper and lengthier climb than for my classmates. I would put this knowledge to use and take action. I had to accept that I had neurologically based conditions that would continue, regardless of how long or how much effort I expended through traditional therapeutic treatment. However, at age 38, it was finally a relief to understand why so many basic tasks were difficult for me. I then could research tutoring and compensatory strategies. This information would, in time, enable me to reframe my experiences, and believe that I was not lazy, careless, resistant to instruction, stupid or self-defeating. I had to redefine myself and wanted others to see me more accurately.

Unfortunately, the antihistamines did not improve my functioning or my state of mind. However, a growing understanding of my neurobiology would serve me well as I experienced some very disturbing symptoms. I awoke one weekend morning to severe nausea, dizziness and an excruciating headache. When I opened my eyes, the room appeared to be circling around me. I got out of bed to go to the bathroom and was unable to go forward as my balance was significantly impaired. My first thought was relief. Erik was with Steve for the weekend and would be spared seeing me in this condition. However, immediately thereafter came the fear that I might be incapacitated for an extended period or even permanently, and unable to care for him. I imagined how a serious illness would impact my parents and felt profoundly sad that my goals would be even more difficult or impossible to attain. I could die! Given the knowledge about my deficits, I believed that I might be having a stroke, an attack of vertigo, or some other neurological illness. I had to be assessed, and pursue treatment as soon as possible. I called a friend and had her drive me to the emergency room. A neurologist was called. After I was examined and tested, it was determined that I had nystagmus and associated benign paroxysmal positional vertigo (BPPV). Nystagmus, a brain disorder, is a miscommunication between the eyes and the brain, and affects the way the brain interprets eye movements. It results in involuntary repetitive eye movements. BPPV, a disorder of the vestibular system, causes dizziness, lightheadedness, loss of balance, nausea, and vertigo with certain head movements. I was given medication for short-term relief, and referred to a physician specializing in my condition. Given the other possibilities, this was good news. The specialist prescribed medication and exercises. The episodes could not be predicted or prevented, but treatment was helpful in shortening the duration of symptoms which I experienced for over two years. During that time, I periodically reminded myself of the reasons for dedicating myself to the goals in which I was invested.

Shortly after I began to integrate the information about my diagnoses, I took the opportunity to communicate what I had learned to Steve. As was our arrangement, he was dropping Erik off after our son had spent the weekend with him and his new family. He told me that Erik would be going with the rest of the family on an island vacation. Since this was a lovely prospect, I thought this would be a good time to provide the news about my diagnoses. Although Steve had moved on, it was important to me that he finally understood the source of some of my difficulties, which had interfered with our marriage. In response to my telling him what I had learned from the newspaper article Carolyn had shown me, he said, “I will tell you when I believe you have learning disabilities.”

Chapter 16

Once I received my diagnosis, I researched all information and resources I could access on learning disabilities in adults. There were a few support groups in my area, and my mother and I attended each one. The individuals in these groups were, for the most part, more severely disabled than I. Although I had hoped to find understanding and a sense of community, the group members and the relatives who accompanied them did not see me as someone with whom they had a mutual interest, nor my challenges as worthy of support. However, I did meet and establish a relationship with Dr. Elaine Fine, a professor at Montclair State College, now Montclair University. She became a mentor, advocate and good friend.

Depressed and disappointed, I was determined to continue my search. During this period, I attended a conference and met Dr. Ted Miller, who was offering services to this population. He himself had a learning disability, which manifested itself most obviously in spelling errors. He was the first of many high-functioning individuals with learning disabilities that I would meet. I was very encouraged to find out that he had earned a doctorate in education, and had established a private practice. We continued our association, and began to lecture together on a variety of subjects relating to learning disabilities. However, these lectures were offered free or at a reduced fee. I would not be able to support myself from the proceeds.

Apart from the emotional impact of my diagnoses, I now had practical decisions to make. It was clear to me, despite the skepticism voiced by virtually everyone but my parents, that I would not be able to handle most entry level jobs. Deficits in fine and gross motor abilities, coordinated movements, balance, calculation, handwriting, sequencing, multitasking, short-term and working memory, and the like ruled out most positions for which I might be eligible. Although it appeared to be a paradox, my best chance was to continue my education, where, despite the results of my comprehensive exam, I had been successful. I had received a great deal of tutoring and instruction in compensatory techniques since that event, which improved my skills. Most importantly, the knowledge of my learning disabilities strengthened my determination to develop my expertise to best assist others with this syndrome. This continued to be the driving force in my life. It was even greater than my overwhelming fear of failure.

I applied to a university that offered a doctoral program in service delivery to students with learning disabilities. The program was only one of the reasons I had decided to apply to that school. It was one of the few universities that was located relatively near to my apartment. This was of the utmost importance as I would not have to relocate to attend. As determined as I was to earn my degree, I was equally determined that Erik would be with his father on a weekly basis. I was hopeful about my chances of being accepted to the university. According to its application materials, I met or exceeded the admission requirements. In the essay asking my motivation for entering the program, I revealed my learning disabilities. I believed that my personal experience and achievements made me an ideal candidate – after all, I had earned a 3.9 GPA with no accommodations. Nevertheless, I was rejected, and advised to reapply the following year. I was not given an explanation for the rejection, which led me to believe that the outcome would be no different in the future. Apart from the great disappointment and feeling of dejection, I was bewildered. I gave their decision a great deal of thought and researched the attitudes and treatment of students with "invisible disabilities." The results were very discouraging. I concluded that, most likely, I had been naive in believing that my learning disabilities would be seen as an asset, regardless of my accomplishments. Eventually, I did get confirmation of discrimination from a very credible source. I then called a family attorney, to ask what action I might take. He informed me that I had no chance of winning this case. Furthermore, he was personally doubtful about granting accommodations to individuals with learning disabilities.

I had endured a year with no progress toward my goal and no earned income. I had to find an alternative path to professional development. After considerable research, I applied to the Learning Disabilities Teacher Consultant program at Montclair State College (now a university). Dr. Warren Heiss, the head of the program, explained that classroom experience as a teacher was required for admission. He then suggested that I apply to their School Psychology program. I decided that I could not risk revealing my learning disabilities. This decision made me angry, frustrated and fearful. The admission standards were very rigorous. There was a group interview, where several faculty members presented candidates with challenging questions that we discussed in their presence. We then had to individually answer an oral question by computer within a very short time.

I left the interview very discouraged, in the midst of a snow storm. When I arrived home, I saw that my son had set our coffee table for a special dinner, candles included. My dad had a dozen roses delivered, congratulating me on the likelihood of my acceptance. As was true so many times throughout my life, I was overwhelmed by their genuinely expressed love and support, despite my many disastrous setbacks. At the same time, I was anxious that I would fail again. I was fearful, and felt guilty about the future and the need for continued sacrifice by my parents and son. (I dried the flowers and saved the accompanying card. When I'm in a nostalgic mood, I take them from my keepsakes box and treasure the memories they evoke.) I had great doubts about being successful without additional time for some of the areas assessed during the interviewing process. Nevertheless, it appeared that I had no choice but to proceed unaccommodated. My strengths outweighed my limitations, and I was accepted! This was wonderful news, but I could not imagine the extent of the challenges that lay ahead. I chose to pursue a degree in School Psychology, with the Learning Disabilities Teacher Consultant curriculum as a second major.

In order to supplement the monies from my estranged husband and parents, I applied for and was granted an assistantship. This required me to test and write reports about youngsters who were being evaluated at our Psychoeducational Center. While my ability to write reports had improved, it continued to be a very time-consuming process. Another source of pressure was the testing procedure. I evaluated children, some of whom were hyperactive or otherwise difficult to assess, in a room with a two-way mirror and a microphone. Outside, two supervisors and the child's parent(s) were watching and listening. I was assigned an excellent tutor for report writing. Dr. Kauffman would review my report and indicate what needed to be changed, but not what the correct version should be. I would then submit as many drafts as was necessary for her to find the work acceptable. Ultimately, I internalized an organizational structure. Unfortunately, my professor, Dr. Jean Levine, would then read the report and often disagree with the phrasing my tutor had endorsed. At the time, students generally used typewriters, not word processors. We were not permitted to turn in any page with a correction. My mother was an excellent secretary and, until I began my doctoral work, she typed, re-typed and again re-typed my papers. After many months had passed, I made an appointment with Dr. Heiss, who had become my mentor. I told him, "My professor and tutor disagree on wording, and I am caught in an endless loop of changes." He resolved the situation, and I had one less obstacle to face. However, even with that resolution, I was still too slow in turning in reports. I felt impelled to reveal "special educational needs," but to no avail! In order to complete my work, I barely slept, and gave up virtually every other activity. This caused me to feel a great sadness and guilt. I had time only to provide Erik with the basics.

I again developed pneumonia, and this time my condition was critical. Once more, I was packed in ice and alternated between consciousness and hallucinations. When I was lucid, I again prayed to be able to continue caring for my son. While I was recovering, my physician warned me that I had not been expected to survive. The pressure to perform academically was intense. However, I still could not see another course to follow. I was not going to be given additional time to complete the reports, as one professor, Dr. Levine, feared this would jeopardize his position. While I was hooked up to an I.V., my mother brought my notes to the hospital and I dictated the material to her.

My assistantship covered tuition for the two semesters normally required to complete a degree. I appealed to my mentor and other supportive faculty members to extend the time period. That would fulfill the purpose of the tuition waiver. I was doubtful that this would be granted, as Montclair State was part of the New Jersey state system. Furthermore, this consideration had never before been granted. In view of my grades and support, I was permitted to continue with my waiver until all requirements were met.

My program had an internship requirement. A portion of the time had to be spent under the supervision of a school psychologist in a high school. In discussing the site's selection, I explained to the administrator, "I discussed my placement with my teenage son. Like every other adolescent I know, he pleaded with me not to be the school psychologist at the high school he is attending." I proudly told Erik, "I made your case," and assured him that my request would be granted. Unfortunately, but typically, there was a snafu and I was assigned to his high school. Once again, I felt powerless to protect my son. However, Erik took the high road, understanding the importance of the placement to my schooling and career. We agreed to pass each other in the school's hallway without so much as eye contact. It was quite bizarre. His friends would call out to me or stop me to chat, but my son and I were the proverbial "ships that pass in the night," and we played our roles flawlessly.

Chapter 17

In spite of the difficulties encountered, I was managing to maintain a 4.0 GPA, and had to complete the final semester. Steve then informed me that he and Carolyn were planning to move into a more expensive home, and the monies to me would cease. He had continued payment beyond the originally agreed-upon time, necessitated by the setback detailed earlier. Therefore, he was within his legal rights to do so. I was devastated and terrified. My greatest concern was the impact that this would have on our son. This arrangement meant that I would have to relinquish my home and temporarily move into my parents' apartment. Erik would then live full time with his father and stepmother. In order to spend any time with him, I would have to drive to his new home, and we would spend Saturdays together. Finally, I would need to take two courses over the accelerated summer session. As one of the courses was not offered until the fall, I asked to take it as an independent study. My professor was entitled to an explanation of the circumstances that justified this consideration. It was extraordinarily painful for me to reveal and re-experience the emotions evoked by my current circumstances before a professor with whom I had no prior contact. In addition, I had great doubts about whether I would be able to fulfill the course requirements over the shortened summer session, as I had never been able to accomplish this. I suffered a profound sense of loss and helplessness over my current situation.

As I have written, my greatest concern was the impact this change was going to have on Erik. Hysterically, I pleaded with Steve, saying, "The conditions of the move could be emotionally harmful to our son." I even enlisted my father to speak with him, as my former husband felt close to my dad. However, all was to no avail. My powerlessness in being unable to keep my child with me, and the loss of Erik in our home, were overwhelming and traumatic. In time, I could see that the new arrangement might benefit Erik. Given all the turmoil we had experienced, I considered that the living conditions at his dad's might be less tumultuous. It was a two-parent, upper-income household. Hopefully, my son would have a good relationship with his two stepbrothers, who were close in age to him.

My parents' apartment was on the New Jersey side of the George Washington Bridge. I would need to travel on heavily trafficked, high-speed roads for evening classes. As my parents were senior citizens, their apartment was rent-controlled. My father, who was ill with Parkinson's disease, was understandably fearful that my presence would cause difficulty. My living there was causing my elderly parents increased stress. I agreed to use the building's rear door, so as to be less likely to be observed. My living situation was extremely painful and, in addition to sadness, I felt great guilt. My mother provided support, saying, "As completing this final term is something that you have to do, we will find a way to accomplish the task." She drew a calendar of the days until the end of the semester, and crossed each one off when I returned to their apartment from school. I earned my certificate as a school psychologist and experienced some short-term relief, but again, no celebration. Upon my graduation, the head of my program said, "Despite your academic accomplishments, you will have difficulty functioning as a traditional school psychologist." I knew that she was correct. At that time, testing and report writing were the primary roles of a school psychologist. While the content of my reports was good, the organization and typing took too much time. Nevertheless, I was again faced with the necessity of finding a job. My colleague, Dr. Miller, offered me a full-time position in his practice. While I was grateful, concerns about our professional compatibility had arisen in the time that we had worked together. In addition, my salary would be minimal, at least to start. Nevertheless, I had to support myself and find employment quickly, so I accepted his offer.

As I previously wrote, my colleague had earned a doctorate in education, despite having an undiagnosed learning disability. He had a small practice in suburban Philadelphia, where he provided various services to individuals with "learning differences," as he called them. While my role involved testing, there were far fewer individuals than I would have been assigned in a school setting, the individuals were adults, and the testing was less comprehensive. As I would be relocating from New Jersey, I would need to find affordable housing. Shirley

Tinsley, the secretary in his practice, lived near the office. She was married with two teenage children, one of whom was in a wheelchair. Her husband was a salesman who did a great deal of traveling. That summer, she was planning on attending a church conference which was being held in another state. As we had become friendly, she suggested that I stay in her home to be there for her daughters. The brief stay expanded into years. I grew to love each family member and enjoyed their company. However, the only room for me was a den where everyone gathered to watch TV. I generally was ready for bed several hours before they were. I tried to keep my eyes open at night, and was exhausted in the mornings. I continued to visit with Erik on Saturdays, but it was now an interstate trip. As I had done before, I treated him to video games and lunch, then took him home. I then returned to my adopted family. The round trip was incredibly difficult. My eye strain was so severe that I had to close my eyes at every light until reaching the turnpike, where my anxiety would be just short of unbearable. During this period, I suffered yet another profound and unexpected loss. My beloved brother-in-law, Marc, suddenly died at the age of 50. He had been a big brother to me since I was a child. I was devastated, and continue to feel the absence of him to this day.

A benefit of my position was that my employer had a relationship with a local psychologist. Dr . Jeffrey Cone had a large practice providing services to individuals who had learning disabilities. I had been seeking a psychologist who would serve as supervisor for my doctoral internship. I needed this to become licensed. An arrangement was made, and I learned a great deal during our weekly meetings. In addition, Dr. Cone wrote a letter, recommending me for the subsequent application to my doctoral program. He offered to be a member of my doctoral committee, and said I could approach his clients for the research I would have to conduct. I worked for my employer until financial constraints and professional differences prompted me to seek another position. I applied for a job in the Disability Center at a New Jersey university. During the interview, I disclosed my disabilities, and was told that my condition posed no problem. The school had several campuses and I was also told that a decision was pending as to my placement. In the interim, I would be traveling between campuses. Not knowing where I would ultimately be employed, I again moved into my parents' apartment, for what I believed would be a short term. I really enjoyed providing tutoring, counseling and assessment. However, driving between the campuses, particularly at night, was proving to be intensely stressful.

During this time, I received my copy of a newsletter from the National Association of School Psychologists. A doctoral program in Neuropsychology with a specialization in Learning Disorders was being offered at a Pennsylvania university. The area of instruction and training was exactly what I had been seeking. In addition, the structure of the program was such that I could, hopefully, make it work. Placement tests would be given, and if I did well on those exams, I would receive credit for previous graduate work. I would then have to complete four semesters of classes over two summers. I was very excited while reading the description of the courses. They seemed very interesting (with the exception of statistics), and would even better prepare me to work with my students. An internship and a dissertation could be completed locally. I remember telling my parents: "I can do this!" Such a burst of confidence was extremely rare for me. I wrote for additional information and was provided with a list of areas to study for the placement test.

Chapter 18

At about the same time, my parents were invited to a friend's retirement party. There, they met Dr. Leo Lippman. He had just been given a grant to research individuals with developmental disabilities at Rutgers University. My parents told him about my involvement in the field, and he was eager to meet with me. I thought that Dr. Lippman would be a good contact. We scheduled an appointment at his home, which was located in a town adjacent to my parents' apartment. Shortly after we began sharing information, we established a rapport. He was a very intelligent, well-informed and sensitive person. I was comfortable enough to disclose my personal as well as professional life story. We decided that I would travel to Rutgers about once a month to have lunch and discuss matters of mutual interest. This continued for over a year and was tremendously valuable to me. During the second summer of our friendship, he and his wife took an extended vacation. On their return, Leo told me that he had become very ill while away, and been diagnosed with a brain tumor. The tumor was surgically removed, he was given a good prognosis and returned to work. I was very concerned about his health, and had missed our lunches, so I quickly arranged a meeting. We saw each other for several months, during which time Leo expressed great support for my application to doctoral programs. On what was to be the final visit to Rutgers (unbeknownst to me), I requested that Leo write me a recommendation to my doctoral program. He was initially concerned about providing this as he had not been one of my professors, but I told him it could be a more informal endorsement. He then graciously crafted a beautiful supportive letter (which I have kept and cherish). As I was leaving, his colleague told me that the cancer had aggressively metastasized, significantly impeding his performance. Leo had been told that this was his last day at Rutgers. I was shocked, deeply pained, and incredibly grateful that he had written the recommendation under those circumstances. I was determined to visit him at his home as often as possible, despite his location, and did so until a short time before his death. On what was to be our last visit, Leo, ever the gentleman, insisted on walking me to my car. I somehow knew that I would not be seeing him again.

His wife, Eleanor, invited me to the memorial service, held in his backyard. His family and many friends were there, and Eleanor invited each one to share memories. Every person described Leo in virtually the same way, as a man above men. My parents had accompanied me, and were offering comfort, as I was devastated by this loss. Sobbing and almost blinded by tears, I heard Eleanor call my name. Completely unprepared, I stumbled to the front of the group, and found that the words flowed. Unaware until after my short speech, I had more or less expressed what those before me had said. Sharing my loss with this community had provided some support. We had temporarily re-created Leo by bearing witness to his unique goodness of mind and heart.

I began to complete the application material, and to study for the placement exam. This would require an interview, and most of the placement test. The statistics portion would be given after acceptance, to determine if any deficiencies would necessitate additional coursework. I was assured that my score on the statistics test would determine my level of proficiency. It would not be used as a criterion for selection. Graduate Record Examination (GRE) scores had to be submitted as well. As noted earlier, I had previously studied for the GRE and Miller Analogies tests, and done very well on both. I was told that there was not enough time for me to retake these examinations for the upcoming semester. The admissions committee would accept my dated scores. At a later time, I would be informed if the tests needed to be retaken.

Friends who had completed doctoral work advised me to request an informational interview with the faculty of my program. I was granted this interview, and it was the first of many trips I would make to the school. Even the forecast of a severe storm and lengthy drive did not dissuade me from my scheduled session. I was very enthused about the program, and given much appreciated support by the faculty. Before leaving, I called my parents and shared my excitement with them.

I scheduled a second trip to take the statistics portion of the placement test. Subsequently, I was thrilled to learn of my acceptance, and shocked about placing out of the first level statistics course. Shortly before I left to begin my semester, my cousin and mentor, Dr. Richard Fertel, had configured a luggable computer (precursor to the laptop) for me. I had mastered Bank Street Writer, one of the earliest and most basic word processing programs. Rich had installed Word Perfect, which was much more powerful and complicated. Always one to have the greatest of confidence in my abilities, he assured me that I could quickly master the complex program.

Chapter 19

As the beginning of classes approached, I packed my clothes, books, paperwork, and documentation of my learning disabilities with great excitement and trepidation. I had a friend, Dr. Debra Stevens, who had earned a doctorate in psychology from the University of Chicago. She knew and prepared me for some of the challenges that lay ahead. On the morning of my trip, Debra presented me with an adorable stuffed lamb we named Baba. He was to be my co-pilot, and provide company, as the fly did for Lindbergh on his monumental flight. I had asked my parents and son to each make a tape of encouragement that I could play before leaving, during my trip, and while at the university. I also had recorded the texts I was studying for the placement exams. I strapped myself and Baba in, inserted a tape, and took off. The trip went smoothly, and many hours later I reached my destination. I vividly recall arriving in the school's parking lot, and putting in the tapes that my parents and Erik had recorded. Tearful, and questioning my decision to take this on, I began to feel my loved ones were with me, as I listened to their voices. I was facing the challenge for which my entire adulthood had been a preparation. Their messages shored up my courage. Unsure of the outcome, I had to honor my family members' sacrifices and faith in me. Determined to do my very best and to persevere, I opened the door to the administration building, and stepped through to my future.

Shortly after arriving, I completed the balance of the placement test. At the conclusion of many hours of testing, a gathering had been planned for the incoming students. I knew that my attendance was expected. This celebration was an important opportunity to meet my peers, and begin to establish a relationship with my professors. However, I was physically, emotionally and cognitively depleted. While my fellow students unwound at the party, I drank the glass of wine I had brought, and immediately fell asleep, alone in the dorm. The following day, I learned that my placement score again indicated no deficiencies. Unlike the results on the statistics placement test, this score was not completely unexpected.

Despite my strong performance in the statistics portion of the placement test, it was many years since I had taken any courses in the subject, and statistics never was a strong suit. Therefore, I had prepared for the statistics portion of the placement test and was a very experienced and proficient test taker. Nevertheless, I understood that I needed a full semester refresher course. I expressed my intention to take this first level statistics course to the professor teaching the course. I told Dr. Peter Baker that I understood this plan would entail an additional cost in time and money. I was assured that this was unnecessary, and told to register for the more advanced level, offered during the second semester.

Registration for classes was extremely stressful. Students gathered en masse. There was the usual confusion, lack of preparation and information, and other problems. As difficult as it was, we all had previous experience with this procedure. However, the first day of classes brought news of an incident that we were unprepared for and that shook us all. We learned that one of our peers had suffered a severe seizure, that she had stopped breathing and was rushed from class to a local hospital. Through the student grapevine, I was told that this was the first seizure she had suffered. Upon recovering, she would not be returning to class. We speculated that the pressure of what we had experienced so far, and what we knew would be expected of us, could be life-threatening. I felt deeply empathic for this student I had never met. Although I was chastened by this news, if anything, my determination was bolstered by it.

I understood that developing a working knowledge of Word Perfect as soon as possible was essential. My excitement at creating draft documents was short-lived, as I was unable to save what I had written. Many documents that I painstakingly composed were lost, due to my misunderstanding of the software. Once I had mastered that procedure, an incompatibility between my computer and printer had to be rectified. By the time all of the aforementioned was resolved, final exams were upon us. At this time of excruciating pressure, I received the dreaded message, "FATAL ERROR." My computer had to be shipped back for repair to its manufacturer in Ohio. Although at a great disadvantage now, I had saved my work on floppy discs. I therefore was free to use the school's computers to complete my work. However, students who did not own a computer had, in advance of final exams, scheduled almost all available time. Fortunately, a few of my fellow students took pity on me, and allowed me to use their computers, once they finished their work. Much to my amazement and relief, I completed the first semester in a state of exhausted exhilaration, earning an "A" average. This had been achieved without any accommodations, as I was advised during my placement interview not to reveal my disabilities. Of course, this evoked a great deal of anger, pain and fear in me. However, having previously encountered discrimination, I believed the advice was sound.

As the second semester approached, I was extremely anxious about the advanced statistics course I was about to begin. On the first day of class, Dr. Baker asked us to raise our hands if we understood various statistical terms. The students who had taken the first level course all raised their hands after each term was announced. Only my hand remained down. Dr. Baker then said to me, "You don't belong in this class." I replied, "I agree." Fortunately, I had overheard that fellowship students in the graduate department were providing free tutoring. (I received a good deal of valuable information about university resources by chance.) I immediately registered for Monday through Friday sessions, throughout my entire semester. The tutoring was essential for me to pass statistics, and continue with the program. I was and remain so very grateful for the excellent support.

Chapter 20

Shortly after my arrival home, I received a call from Dr. Cone. He informed me that there was an opening for a psychologist to establish a program for students with learning disabilities, at a college preparatory school in suburban Philadelphia. This appeared to be a wonderful opportunity for several reasons. As always, I was eager to enlighten the students, lessen their burden, and expand their options. I had not yet been given the responsibility of establishing a program, and saw this as a chance for professional development. The location promised two benefits. First, I would reside in the state where I was completing my doctoral work, resulting in a significant tuition reduction. Secondly, Dr. Cone had previously volunteered to serve on my doctoral committee. As he had a private practice, I hoped that his clients might be willing to serve as subjects for my dissertation research.

I was looking forward to relocating to Pennsylvania, and asked Shirley if she had any information about garden apartments near the school and her home. Fortunately, she did. A friend of hers was living nearby, and said that her complex was very well-maintained. Upon visiting the Radcliffe House, I was impressed with the grounds, as well as the apartments. I spoke with several of the tenants, who were very satisfied with their living arrangements. Feeling excited about my new home and position, I signed the lease and planned to move.

I prepared to assume my new role, with the naivety of one who has not yet attempted to establish a controversial program in an educational institution. Unfortunately, I found that many parents were unreceptive to my information if their children's testing results indicated any problem or deficiency. Much to my shock and disappointment, this was even true of parents who were professionals in the field of special education! After several months, with my disillusionment intensifying, I was approached by the principal. He informed me that the school counselor felt overburdened by her caseload. I would be expected to share her duties as well as to continue with my own, which included teaching a course in psychology. It was clear that this would significantly limit my availability to perform the primary duties for which I was hired. I was told that a refusal would result in a failure to renew my contract. This created a great conflict. I knew, from past experience, that it would be difficult to find employment to accommodate my learning disabilities. It could necessitate being financially dependent on my parents again. They were then living on a fixed income, and I was desperate to avoid burdening them. I agonized over my decision, but ultimately, I could not subject my students to the disappointments and injustices that they and I had faced. Had I remained there, I would not be honoring the sacrifices my parents had made. I assumed that the colleague who had informed me about the position would find a place for me on his staff; he would continue his commitment to serve on my doctoral committee. However, when my phone messages were not returned, I was devastated on a personal and professional level.

I was adrift. At that time, I had one summer of classes remaining. I again had to process neuropsychological texts at an accelerated pace. I did not have a problem with the conceptual aspect of learning. However, applying the knowledge to the testing situation proved to be a considerable challenge. We were required to administer a comprehensive neuropsychological battery to each other, while being observed by our classmates. Following the directive given to me earlier, I had not revealed my learning disabilities to faculty, other than to my primary advisor; nor had I informed my fellow students. I panicked. As a testee, I knew that there were tasks that would cause me great difficulty. In fact, there was one item tapping spatial memory that I was completely unable to do. As the timed minutes passed, my frustration and humiliation grew, along with my fellow students' joking references to me as brain-damaged. They carried this epithet out of the classroom and into the cafeteria. I laughed along with them, as I had learned to do so many times before, while trying to suppress my emotional devastation and anger.

We next had to recruit and administer the test to several youngsters, report the findings to our classmates for review, and submit the reports to our professor. In addition, we were required to tape a testing session. I experienced challenges similar to the ones I previously had with my peers, as I administered my battery before the unblinking, unforgiving eye of the video camera. High budget movies probably have fewer re-takes than mine did, as I subjected my classmate's children to mastering my craft. I could have sold the outtakes to a television comedy network, but I was far from finding humor in the situation.

As with the neuropsychological component of the program, we were expected to apply the statistical concepts to problem solving. This would be through the use of software. At first, I believed that this would greatly simplify the projects. Unfortunately, this was not the case. My limited grasp of the subject matter, coupled with perceptual-motor deficits that resulted in slow and inaccurate keyboarding, caused me great difficulties and enormous stress. At this point I had no choice but to reveal my disabilities to Dr. Baker. He gave me an incomplete for the assigned projects that I would then be permitted to complete at home. As far as my request for a time extension for in-class testing, he responded by allowing everyone in the class to have additional time. This enabled me to earn the grade commensurate with my knowledge, which was of primary concern. However, his rationale that this would then "be fair to all" was frustrating. It indicated a lack of understanding of my particular need for accommodation. This lack of understanding had also been evidenced by some of my friends and family members. They did, and still do, insist, "All people have weaknesses as well as strengths." This comment appears to be well-meaning. However, the impact of my challenges has been considerably more widespread and severe than the impact experienced by those who attempt to "reassure" me. Outwardly, I may appear to accept what I hear. At best, I am resigned to the lack of understanding. However, I often feel frustrated, sad and angry. As both a student and a professional, my requests to accommodate learning disorders were frequently seen as invalid, in contrast to those with sensory or motor disabilities. Accommodations for sensory and motor deficits are also less controversial, because the issue of lowering academic standards is less frequently raised. However, students with visible disabilities may also encounter the uninformed perspective that they are not "college material."

Chapter 21

Once I had mastered my doctoral coursework, I anticipated being notified that I had matriculated, and could begin the next phase of my program. However, that did not occur. Certain that there had been an oversight, I made an appointment with my department head. He informed me that I had never taken the Graduate Record Examination as part of the application procedure. I responded that my scores were on file, and reminded him that re-taking the examination was presented as an option, since I had done so well on the original testing. I was to have been informed if a second test was necessary. In addition, the examination was to serve as a predictor of success. I had completed all of my coursework with an "A" average. Our discussion proceeded in a reasonable manner, and I was then permitted to matriculate.

At that point in my life, I had several priorities. The first was to find some means of supporting myself. A colleague had told me there was a part-time position for a psychologist at a local college. The position entailed assessing service delivery for students with learning disabilities, head injuries, and medical conditions which affect cognition. I was also to provide services. My first requirement was to establish a weekly team meeting, when students and administrative issues would be discussed. A second requirement was to read any documentation a student provided, and conduct a clinical interview. When more information was needed, I was to select the instruments to administer, as well as to score and interpret the testing. Third, I would be presenting inservices to faculty, consulting with individual faculty members as needed, devising workshops for students, and contributing to grant writing. It was an extensive list, but I was told that eventually I would be employed full time. I was prepared and enthusiastic, but uncertain about whether to reveal my disabilities. I strongly believed that it would be helpful in building rapport with the students. However, I was fearful of facing discrimination, and decided to spend some time in the environment before making that decision. I would, thereby, forgo the possibility of accommodations. Nevertheless, I was in constant fear of exposure, which could result in termination. I reassured myself that, with additional time and effort, I could succeed in a job that drew heavily on my strengths and minimally on my limitations. I had learned to compensate quite well and would observe the way that others who were far more organized than I structured their tasks.

I began to do some tutoring in my home to help cover expenses, and could not imagine that this would introduce me to my future husband. Tenants told the building superintendent, Nick, that I provided tutoring for adults with special needs.. Uncomfortable about meeting my "unknown" client by myself, I was told that mutual friends would accompany "Rick" to my apartment. At the appointed time, I opened my door to see our friends and the building superintendent. My first thought was that it was inconvenient for him to be stopping by, just when I was expecting my new client. It took me some seconds to realize that he was the client! As we became acquainted, Nick told me that spelling had always presented a problem for him. He was looking for assistance to accurately fill out work slips. In further discussion, Nick revealed that as a young child, he had suffered a severe closed head injury in an auto accident, and was given the last rites. At the time, Nick made what was thought to be a full recovery. Therefore, his difficulties in reading and spelling were believed to be unrelated to the accident. It was assumed that Nick wasn't bright. Unfortunately, as a student in Catholic school, it was also assumed that he wasn't sufficiently motivated and Nick repeatedly faced humiliation. He would be asked to squat down in the front of the classroom with arms outstretched and laden with books. The class would then be asked, "Do you want to be like Nick?" His younger siblings also attended that school. When a nun slapped one of them, his mother transferred all of the children to public school.

The next school Nick attended was rife with racial conflicts. He was assaulted several times before again being transferred to a vocational school. Apart from his special needs, which were never identified as such, Nick had to help support his family. He therefore worked through the night, and attended school during the day. The only classes where Nick excelled were the shop courses. He told me that early in his life, he saw himself as a "worker bee," who was only good with his hands. Not surprisingly, he was unaware of how intelligent and creative he was.

When we first met, Nick was approaching 40 years old, and had read only one book in his life. While I had read very many books, I owned only textbooks. Nick bought me my first leisure read. He encouraged me to purchase books that I would enjoy reading and treasure. We both began to build our libraries.

As we continued with our tutoring sessions, his goals became more ambitious. Nick had become interested in continuing his education. With my assistance in obtaining accommodations, he enrolled in a math class at a local community college, and did very well. He intended to take additional courses, but his part-time business was absorbing a great deal of his time. Along with the growth of his business, our relationship was entering a new phase. I was beginning to admit to myself that I was attracted to Nick. I had never met anyone who was as eager to learn as he was. His excitement was exhilarating. Nick was also very kind, had a great personality, was masterful in the kitchen, and what we might call a "hunk."

Each weekend I traveled to New Jersey to assist my mother in caring for my dad. It was agonizing to see how his every movement was painful and required great effort. My father was trained as a pharmacist. He advanced to regional sales manager in a family-owned pharmaceutical company. Besides being very bright and wonderfully kind and generous, he had terrific fine and gross motor skills. Dad greatly enjoyed sports, particularly golf. A bittersweet memory was the enormous pride I felt at the way he had carried himself. His walk and stance seemed to express his dignity, self-respect and unassuming confidence. I would return from these trips absolutely drained. As I walked into the entranceway of my building, Nick would "just happen to be passing by," or so I thought. He offered to take me out for dinner, and serve as a sounding board. I was very grateful for his attention and generosity, but unaware that he had any interest in me other than as a mentor and friend. After more than a year of tutoring, I told Nick that there was something we had to discuss, at the end of our session. We were in his apartment at the time. It was a brutally hot summer night, and I could not afford air conditioning. Much to his surprise, I asked for a glass of wine. Gathering my courage, I revealed that my growing attraction to him was affecting my ability to concentrate on our tutoring. I offered to find him another tutor. Nick then revealed that he shared my feelings. He had been reluctant to express them, as he did not believe they would be reciprocated. I did not anticipate that response. Despite what he said, I did not think that our relationship could be sustained. I was considerably older, of a different religion, and had an advanced degree. In contrast, Nick had limited opportunities to gain much from his formal education. Nevertheless, we had many qualities in common - love of learning, shared values, mutual respect, admiration, as well as an intense attraction. In addition, our areas of deficits differed, so we complemented each other.

Chapter 22

Nick provided entertainment, companionship and support, as I entered the next phase of my doctoral studies. I had to arrange for an internship. Having me as an intern offered an institution both benefits and disadvantages, as compared to students who were completing all their graduate studies in one university. Those students would be spending their internship in one setting. I, on the other hand, had served as an intern in my Masters and School Psychology programs. This meant that I had fewer hours to fulfill as a doctoral intern. What I did have to offer was many years of professional experience. I selected the internship site which appeared to provide the best training in my specialization of neuropsychology. However, this facility predominantly provided services to children. I had devoted most of my professional life to serving adults. I disclosed my inexperience with the instruments that were used for testing. My advisors assured me that I could take my time in becoming acquainted with the materials. I would not be required to test until I felt prepared to do so. However, as space was limited, there had been no provision made for my office or testing equipment, unlike the arrangements for my colleagues, who had twelve-month internships.

I had to find offices that were temporarily vacant, and available testing materials, in order to conduct evaluations and write reports. In addition, as this was summer, I was assigned two supervisors, so each could take time off for vacations. They did provide limited input when I submitted drafts of my reports. However, I only received the entire critique of my work after all my reports had been written. Therefore, I could not fully benefit from my supervisors' feedback. Not surprisingly, their comments indicated that I should continue my internship beyond that semester. I did not believe that this was reasonable, as I had not been given timely supervision, or a workable environment. In addition, the Dean of the college where I was employed had allowed me to work only one day a week during my internship. He was expecting me to resume my prior schedule when classes began in the fall.

While struggling with this dilemma, I was informed that my parents were ill. They were about to be hospitalized in separate New Jersey facilities. I was the only family member who would take charge of their situation. When I informed a supervisor of this, she expressed her disapproval of my temporary leave. I knew that this would further jeopardize my standing. However, there was no option in my mind other than to assume this responsibility. On my return, totally exhausted, I managed to complete the revisions on my reports. When they were submitted, I told my supervisors that I was not prepared to continue my unpaid internship, as I had not received timely feedback. I was willing to discuss the issue further with my university doctoral advisor and representatives from professional organizations, if necessary. Fortunately, it was not necessary. When my reports were re-evaluated, I was given an A.

In June 1995, I celebrated Father's Day with my dad, as I had done every year since being adopted. Although his mobility was severely impaired, he insisted on walking me to the door and said, "I'm really glad to see you looking so well, Malke." As we left, I said to Nick, "I don't think I will see my father alive after this visit," and I turned out to be right. My mother and I were devastated by this loss. I was particularly saddened that he had not lived to see me earn my doctorate. Dad had been one of my greatest supporters, and rejoiced at all my accomplishments. When I was about to embark on a new venture, he would say, "Go get 'em tiger." I carried on that tradition by telling my students to "go get 'em tiger," and silently dedicated their successes to him.

Following my father's death, issues arose among the immediate family members concerning distribution of assets. As a result, a division that had existed from the time of my parents' marriage widened irreparably. Unfortunately, it became necessary for me to protect my mother's financial wellbeing. While I was able to do that, mom paid an unjust and enormous emotional price, as did I, because her pain became mine. Nevertheless, she did quite well for the first year after becoming a widow. There were many arrangements to be made and initially she was able to handle it all.

I continued to keep abreast of current research, and maintained membership in professional associations, enabling me to engage in the best possible practice. I believed that the American Psychological Association

(APA) had the power, the recognition and the resources to advance the causes of critical importance to the population I served. Therefore, I was greatly interested to read in the APA newsletter about the establishment of a group of psychologists who would focus on issues pertinent to disabled psychologists, as well as disabled individuals in the general population. Enthusiastically, I applied. After the date for selection had passed with no notification, I contacted the administrative assistant. I was informed that my material was never received, and that the time for submission had passed. Deeply disappointed, I was determined to reapply when applications were again being accepted.

My participation at that time would have been difficult due to unfolding circumstances. Unbeknownst to me, my mother's mood and coping capabilities had been buoyed by the unrealistic expectation of a family reconciliation. She anticipated that the memorial service for my father, which was held a year after his death, would bring this about. When this did not occur, she progressively became deeply depressed and anxious, and found it difficult to live alone. As she did not want to leave her apartment, we hired the woman who had assisted her in the final months of my father's life. We also arranged for counseling. Nick and I spent the majority of our weekends visiting my mother. Prior to our arrival, she would ask us to accompany her on various errands. However, once we were there, mom never felt well enough to go out. Having been highly selective about her clothing throughout her life, my mother was rarely if ever satisfied with our choices. We would come home exhausted, frustrated and worried. I had little energy for my vocational and educational duties. After about six months, my mother began to improve, and we strongly encouraged her to join the Senior Citizen's Center. There, she participated in both art and poetry groups. Although mom had previously demonstrated her creativity in painting and home decor, I now was greatly impressed by her poetry.

While my mother was enjoying satisfaction and success through her written expression, I was struggling. I believed that the many research papers I had written prepared me well for the dissertation process. However, I completely underestimated what the project entailed. The first step was to select a topic. I had an interest in studying executive functions (attention, concentration, memory, organization, initiation and regulation of behavior, etc.). However, Dr. Carl Remington, my advisor, specialized in the vocational component of schooling. Therefore, I selected an area in that domain to research. I had overcome, to a significant extent, my difficulties in the organization of written expression. However, this work was far more demanding than anything I had done so far. It required many rewrites, and I was at a significant disadvantage in working off campus. While taking my classes, I had learned how valuable the exchanges were with other students. Much information about professors, courses and resources was primarily available through discussions, group study sessions or overheard conversations. I had very little access to this critically valuable incidental learning. Unfortunately, none of the students in my program lived anywhere near me. Their schedules and mine made communication by phone or email difficult.

Another difficulty of off-campus work was reaching my advisor by phone, and receiving timely feedback. Faculty members who serve as advisors have many additional responsibilities. Time spent in their offices is limited, and students on site have more direct access to them. I did avail myself of two out-of-state resources. The first was a statistics tutor I had engaged for my class work, Martin Cain. We had been co-workers at the beginning of my studies, and our tutorial relationship, as well as friendship, continued when I moved to Pennsylvania. The second resource was my cousin, Dr. Richard Fertel. Although a doctoral advisor in another field, his knowledge of the process, and strength in research design, as well as in written communication, was invaluable. He also provided a great deal of morale support.

I usually felt overwhelmed when receiving my advisor's recommendations for revision on my drafts. One moment of utter discouragement is clear in my memory. I was required to research and summarize literature that was pertinent to my study. Nick and I went to the local university, and copied every article that appeared relevant. After reading voluminous material, I excerpted what appeared essential, and reworked my section many times, until it seemed to be well organized. I was devastated by my advisor's comments. Unaware of certain guidelines, I had to virtually redo my entire section. I felt totally drained, discouraged and unable to continue. Nick encouraged me to go on. He said that I must not give up, having invested so much of myself in this project. He reminded me of all the students that I was determined to help. And go on and on and on we did.

Chapter 23

Nick's part time business was thriving. We had decided that he should leave his position and be self-employed. In order for this to happen, we had to purchase a home with an unattached garage that could be used as a workshop. We also had to be married for Nick to be covered under my health insurance at work. After months of intense searching, we found a "handyman's special," which met our basic requirements. Over the period of one week, we were married, moved into our home, and Nick was providing services on a full-time basis. Given the tight time constraints, we chose to have a Quaker ceremony. The only attendees were our mothers, who were in separate residences. As is true in the Quaker tradition, there was no one officiating at our ceremony. Nick wanted to have the reception in our home, but I did not agree. We had no opportunity to do a thorough cleaning, much less to renovate or decorate. We never did schedule our celebration.

As I predicted, Nick's enterprise flourished. He was swamped with clients, and greatly enjoyed all the benefits of ownership. Loving and appreciating him as I did, his success was deeply gratifying to me. Nick was finally able to demonstrate his wealth of talent. A second benefit allowed him to take care of some errands, as his clients lived a short distance from our home. However, a disadvantage of our situation was that it left relatively little time for home improvement. We were both exhausted at the end of the day, and a portion of the weekend was devoted to family visits and errands, as well as to my doctoral work. The condition of the house proved to be a much greater problem to me than I had anticipated. Having an attentional disorder, I had been accustomed to living in a small, very well-organized apartment. Everything could be easily found. My new residence had four floors and a number of small rooms, with very little closet space. The time required to repair or renovate the 90-year-old house got longer, due to the difficulty of finding suitable replacement parts. Surfaces were, of course, not composed of materials that are easily cleaned, but of wood, and were well-worn. I found myself completely overwhelmed, depressed, and anxious. Nick was sympathetic and doing all he could in his many areas of responsibility. We bolstered each other's mood, and assured ourselves that, once we became accustomed to the new routine, we would make considerable progress.

My dissertation was significantly adding to the stress of incorporating major home improvements into our lives. The doctoral process required several defenses of my research. These entailed description of my proposal, my collection of data, the statistics used, and interpretation of my results to my committee. After several cancellations of one of my defense dates, Nick decided to cheer me up by installing new kitchen counters. For the first time, when remodeling, he decided to disassemble our kitchen, before purchasing supplies. On October 24, 1997, we left for Home Depot, anticipating that this would be a trip no different from the hundreds we had taken before. However, the events that followed were life-altering.

On our way home, we were involved in a head-on collision, with the driver impacting us at about 55 m.p.h. I recall seeing the driver approaching us with his hands raised in the air! After the crash, my first terrifying memory is of Nick saying that he could not breathe. We were taken to the hospital by ambulance and separated. The driver who had caused the accident was assigned to the cubicle next to mine. Nick's quick reaction time saved this driver from decapitation, and he was walking around the emergency room. I did not know Nick's condition, or even if he was alive. Intense fear and anger welled up in me. I felt that I might lose complete control of myself should Nick be seriously injured. After many hours, it was determined that neither of us had sustained a serious injury. We felt incredibly lucky. Unfortunately, that was an illusion. In fact, the accident upended almost every aspect of our lives.

About ten days after the accident, Nick suddenly found that he was unable to put any weight on his left leg. He began to suffer excruciating pain from his back down through the leg. At about the same time, I began to see what appeared to be a "veil" of black specks (scotomas). They appeared to my left eye and moved back and forth over my entire field of vision. Testing to determine the cause of my visual symptoms was a prolonged process. In some instances, the procedures were very painful, such as a spinal tap. Even worse, in a research study, magnets were applied to my head and progressively stronger electrical charges were triggered. Ultimately, no diagnosis of my visual condition could be made. Therefore, I had no prognosis. I began to fear that I would become blind. The thought that this could happen while I was traveling to work was terrifying. I temporarily stopped driving, but then had to rely on public transportation. I struggled with the fear that I would have to depend on a stranger to navigate me to safety, while traveling to or walking in the busy city of Philadelphia.

A very short time after the accident, my advisor informed me that I had to schedule the defense of my proposal. I explained that a recent auto accident had caused a number of symptoms that would compromise my performance. I was reassured that consideration would be given to my neurological status. I then scheduled the date for about three weeks after the accident. I was not driving due to my visual deficits, and there was no public transportation available. Nick insisted that he provide that service. He said that his support would be critical (even more so than we could have imagined). Nevertheless, I was torn. As desperately as I wanted him with me, knowing the pain that this would cause him was unbearable. Ultimately, I was unable to convince him to let me search for alternatives, and we set off.

The trip itself was a difficult one, traversing over mountainous roads with virtually no lighting. When we arrived, we were completely exhausted. Of course, I was familiar with the material which comprised my project. However, my memory and organizational abilities were never strengths. These capacities had been further compromised by injuries sustained in the accident. Prior to the collision, I had found it hard to express myself in a concise, organized fashion. Appreciating these limitations, I wrote salient points on index cards. I believed that this would be a consideration afforded to me under the circumstances. Unfortunately, I had not questioned my advisor about what considerations would be acceptable. Midway through my talk, I was told that the defense must be presented with no visual prompts. I panicked, and my tendency to ramble was exacerbated. Looking at the committee members' faces, I could see irritation. When I finished, I was told to wait outside the room where I had defended my work as to whether I had passed. Nick and I held hands, and neither of us could talk. I was overcome by emotions. Anger, anxiety, confusion, frustration and disbelief flooded through me. My heart was pounding, and I was nauseated and dizzy. After what seemed like hours, my advisor emerged from the room. Summoning the courage to look at his face, I saw a smile, and began to relax. Then I heard, "While your presentation is unacceptable, you will be allowed to continue with your dissertation." I felt both relief and discouragement. This wasn't the worst-case scenario. Nevertheless, I didn't experience the confidence I had hoped for, to support me for the challenges that lay ahead.

Chapter 24

Arriving home, I fluctuated between a sense of inertia and a fierce determination to earn my doctoral degree, a goal which had dominated my entire adult life. Nick had disassembled the plumbing and wiring in the kitchen prior to the accident. Therefore, we had no running water there for about two months. This was an extreme inconvenience. Climbing stairs was difficult for us, and Nick was not well enough to do the repair. We did not want to spend the money to hire a contractor, as we were unsure about how our injuries would affect our ability to work. To add to our difficulties, we had numerous appointments with doctors, physical therapists and attorneys. These then led to numerous tests. I was diagnosed with post-concussion syndrome, as well as injuries to my lumbar spine and left knee. As for Nick, he was diagnosed with two herniated discs.

We also had to deal with an ongoing mass of paperwork related to the accident. We learned that we had been given poor advice by our initial legal counsel and insurance representative. This resulted in a large portion of insurance coverage being inaccessible to us. Of course, it also necessitated changing attorneys, and attendant significant delays. Finally, although we both had disability insurance, injuries in Nick's lower back were excluded from coverage, due to an earlier, brief bout with sciatica. As he had no employees, the business came to an abrupt halt. Having moved into the neighborhood a short time before the accident, we hadn't developed any friendships, and had no family nearby to assist us.

Despite my emotional and physical distress, I had to continue my job and dissertation responsibilities. Nick might be unable to work, or able to work only in a limited capacity. I had several obstacles to overcome in earning my degree. The first entailed enlisting subjects to participate in my research. Under ordinary circumstances, this is usually difficult, unless the researcher is in a position to offer subjects a desirable incentive. As I was not a faculty member, there was no direct access to a body of students, nor the opportunity to offer an inducement, such as extra credit. I therefore had to rely on the goodwill of a faculty member. Being fairly new in the school, I did not know many of my colleagues. An even greater impediment at the time was the possibility of a strike. Faculty were understandably reluctant to give me any time in the classroom should a strike be called. If a strike was called, students would be, for the most part, unavailable. Adding to the pressure was the deadline for the completion of my dissertation. I had met a fellow doctoral student who was sympathetic to my plight. Dr. Sonia Lott-Harrison, professor of psychology extraordinaire, enabled me to recruit and assess her students before the strike took place.

I now had hundreds of questionnaires to analyze, and was faced with the challenge of statistical interpretation. The tutor I engaged during my coursework, Martin Cain, had been enormously helpful and generous with his time. We had conducted many of our sessions by phone, as I had moved from New Jersey to Pennsylvania. With data collected, I had arranged for a weekend trip to Martin's home. We intended to spend some time socializing, and then work through the next statistical step. As the weekend progressed, it became obvious that no time was being set aside for work. About an hour before we were to leave, Nick, although very uncomfortable, asked if we could discuss my project. We did spend a short amount of time on one aspect of it, but I realized that Martin's continuing involvement in my doctoral work had to be addressed. On returning home, I agonized over how to proceed. My friendship and degree were on the line. I called him and said that it was understandable if the challenges my committee was creating, as well as his own responsibilities, had become too burdensome. Martin assured me that was not the case. Nevertheless, each time I called, there were prolonged periods before he would respond. It was becoming increasingly awkward and anxiety-provoking, as I had a deadline to meet. During our last conversation, Martin said that he disagreed with a statistical procedure my committee advocated. His reasoning seemed sound, but knowing the members, I did not believe it was in my best interest to suggest another approach. He offered to speak with the committee, but I did not feel this would further my case.

While I did not want to search for another tutor at that time, it seemed the only option. Fortunately, a colleague told me about her tutor. With trepidation, I contacted her. Knowing my struggle to understand statistical concepts, I feared experiencing humiliation and panic. After our first meeting, my fears were allayed. Vivian was wonderful and I quickly became at ease in working with her. I then wrote Martin a letter, saying that his involvement in my research appeared to be straining our relationship, and it seemed best to find other help. I stressed the value of our friendship and my gratitude for all he had done for me. I was confused and pained when my letter met with no reply.

However, I was soon to face a much more devastating situation. My injuries were significantly hampering my ability to process written material, much of which was required both by my doctoral work and my position. My reading speed, internal organization of material, and retention were compromised. Therefore, after the accident, I needed to painstakingly re-read the same material over several times. This impeded not only how long it took me to read material, but to comprehend it as well. Very early on, without conscious awareness, I had developed the technique of reading quickly, to compensate for eye tracking and focusing irregularities. In fact, I had become a rapid, accurate reader. I no longer had my greatest strength. This loss caused me much anguish and anxiety.

When Nick was able to drive me to the train, he did. However, his pain and fatigue were significantly increasing, so I did not want to further burden him. His pain eventually became unbearable, even with the most potent medications and physical therapy. Nick had been strongly opposed to surgery. His father had suffered a similar back injury, and several unsuccessful surgeries had left him incapacitated and in intractable pain. Fearfully, but having no other viable choice, we elected to have the surgery. Fortunately for us, Nick's sister, Barbara, worked for one of the top orthopedic specialists in the country. Through her efforts, Nick was able to receive the best of care from Dr. Richard Balderson. I stayed by his side through the days and nights of his hospitalization. I watched, helpless, as he awoke in agony, post-surgery.

Nick had a prolonged, but ultimately successful recovery. I dreaded leaving him alone when I was at work, but he was able to manage. Upon being released from care by Dr. Balderson, Nick was told that there would be permanent restrictions on his ability to do heavy lifting. This would limit the jobs he could accept. Nevertheless, we were so grateful that the pain was significantly lessened, and there were no signs of paralysis. Nick was referred to a physiatrist, resumed physical therapy, and was injured in the process! Treatment was halted until he recovered from that setback, and another therapist could be found. At this point, we were frightened, but felt that he had no choice but to risk the therapy.

Once Nick had recovered to the point where he was able to drive, we scheduled an appointment with his rehab physician. En route, we were rear-ended by another car. At first, we seemed to have sustained only minor injuries, and Nick was given a release, with restrictions. However, having experienced the previous accident and delay of symptoms, we were far from reassured. In fact, I was soon diagnosed with a second concussion, and the visual disturbances recurred with their previous severity. I also sustained sprains and strains throughout the upper portion of my body, and a compressed nerve which caused excruciating pain in my left thigh. Finally, my left knee was injured. I was afraid to miss work, so my physician wrote prescriptions for valium as a muscle relaxer, codeine for the pain, and an emetic for any nausea produced by the codeine. Somehow, I was able to navigate myself to work, and to function there. Nick and I continued with physical therapy. I was terrified when either of us had to be on the road. Fear constantly threatened to overwhelm me. I had flashbacks to the previous accidents, and could barely suppress a scream when a vehicle came near us. Knowing how anxiety had proven very destructive in my first marriage, I was determined to return to my pre-accident levels and continue with my commitments.

Chapter 25

Devastatingly, Nick's injuries did reoccur. At first, he was again given increasing levels of medication, in the hopes of avoiding a second surgery. Eventually, his pain was so extreme that an operation was again required. We selected a local hospital rather than travel to Philadelphia, as we previously had done. Unfortunately, during the procedure, a piece of disc relocated itself against a nerve in his spine, and the pain was unbearable. Less invasive procedures than a full operation were performed, but they failed. A third surgery was performed by Dr. Balderson, and the pain was greatly lessened. I, however, was struggling with increasing knee pain.

After much hard work, my analyses were completed, and I submitted my dissertation to my advisor for his review. I requested that any questions, concerns or additions regarding, in particular, my statistics, be presented to me prior to the defense. I would then have time to make required changes, without the stress of the presentation exacerbating my dyscalculia (mathematically based learning disability). He informed me that the committee members had read my dissertation, and essentially had approved it. All that was left was to commit the salient material to memory, and defend what I had done. Given the short time left in which to complete my work, I questioned my advisor about applying for an extension. He said that it would not be necessary, as my dissertation had been, in essence, found acceptable.

Two days prior to my defense, Nick and I again made the long journey to the school. I anxiously worked to commit my research to memory, as we wound around the densely foggy, mountainous roads. The following day, I alternated between rehearsal and using every means to calm myself. Nick offered his full support, which bolstered me, as I stepped into the room to present my material. Dr. Remington greeted me, and said that we had to talk. Apparently, there had been some miscommunication, and my committee had not read my material! I panicked almost to the point of muteness, felt faint, and could barely think cogently. However, this was my moment and I began my defense. When we reached the statistical portion of my presentation, I was questioned in great detail about my various approaches. I could hardly stammer an answer. My mind went blank. At one point, I was told by a committee member that my responses were such that the project appeared to be at its inception!

My academic life almost literally "flashed before my eyes." I had begun my undergraduate training over 30 years before, and had resolutely, often in desperation, overcome all obstacles in pursuing my goal. I sacrificed whatever was necessary, as did my family. In doing so, I was able to achieve a 4.0 GPA throughout my doctoral coursework. As I slogged on, there were no indications from my committee members as to what the outcome would be. I was asked to wait outside the room, while they determined my academic and career fate. I was traumatized. As Nick supported me, while dealing with his feelings, we heard laughter coming from the room. Whether related to my presentation or not, their enjoyment made me feel even more ill. I had anticipated going home to a joyous celebration, and now feared that my family would be subjected to yet another deeply felt disappointment. After what seemed like an interminable period of time, Dr.Remington stepped out of the room, and walked down the hallway toward us. He smiled and said, "Congratulations." I was overcome with relief, until he finished his statement. I would be allowed to continue with changes and additional analyses. Once again, while this was not the worst-case scenario, it certainly wasn't the best.

My first problem was obtaining a time extension at this late date. I was told that only my advisor could facilitate this. None of my committee members were permitted to fulfill this function. Initially, I had difficulty locating him, as he was off campus. Ultimately, I contacted him and he had the request approved on the last permissible day. Next, I had to conceptualize, carry out and incorporate the additional analyses into my document. Those tasks accomplished and accepted, I submitted my final draft to the graduate school. The responsibility of that department was to determine if the dissertation's format met the exacting standards of the American Psychological Association's style manual. It was approved. I believed once again that I was at the finish line, but there were still several more challenges to meet.

I forwarded my dissertation to my committee. It was returned to me with the comment that the format did not follow APA style. I was referred to a page in the APA manual to correct my draft. I repeatedly reviewed the page, but could not find where I differed from the approved standard. I brought my dissertation back to the graduate school and had it re-reviewed (although it had already passed). The administrator in charge was also unable to find the discrepancy. My committee would give me no instruction, other than to refer me to the page number in the APA manual. The clock was ticking, and I was panicking. I had laboriously typed the dissertation on my word processor. However, in desperation, I contacted a secretary in a department other than mine, who had experience in typing APA documents. I asked her to retype my work, and she expressed reluctance for several reasons. I literally begged her and offered to pay any reasonable fee. I wasn't certain that my committee would accept her document, but could think of nothing else to do. She agreed and the format was found acceptable.

I was now at the final phase of the process, ordinarily a matter of protocol. A representative from the Graduate School had to sign off on the work. Again, unfortunately, the staff member who held that responsibility was ill, and about to take a leave of absence. The temporary replacement did not hold a doctoral degree. My committee stated that this was required to fulfill that responsibility. A fully credentialed individual was not scheduled to assume this and other duties until after my extension expired. Eventually, the issue was resolved. At the end of 1998, I was awarded my degree. I had dreamed and planned for the time that I would walk down that aisle. Friends and family would share my triumph and joy. However, the prolonged, painful process had taken a toll on my health and my spirit. I did not attend my graduation ceremony, the acknowledgement of a lifelong achievement. As my home was under renovation, it seemed best to postpone a celebration of my marriage, home ownership and degree.

My achievement was, however, recognized in the most meaningful of ways. My son presented me with the following poem:

WITH A STEP

"The waves of her hair rolled across her eyes like a blonde ocean
She was a little girl and in front of her was the world
They told her she was too young, too small yet to walk
She bumped into chairs, fell on her nose, bruised her knees
Soon, she was running like the wind
It began with a step
Now the curls kissed her shoulders lightly
She was a girl with a dream
They said she was too shy to play with the children in the water
She inched forward, each foot seeming an anchor
She stepped from the sand towards the lake
Soon, she was running like the wind
It began with a step
Like a sheet of strawberry silk, her hair flowed from the nape of her neck to meet her back
She was a young adult seeking a hidden truth
They told her it would be too difficult a challenge,
She studied, agonized, sought guidance, feared she could not go on
She passed and failed, but always she learned
Soon she was running like the wind
It began with a step

Her tresses lay shorter then, just topping a fringe of eyelash
She was a woman, mature, with each breath more sure
They told her she could not succeed, her goal unreachable
She struggled, was battered, knew losses, but fought her way through
Soon, she was running like the wind
It began with a step
The clouds above are jealous of the silver lining which now streaks her mane
Showered with kisses, she is Dr. and Mrs.
Some will say she has taken too long,
What can lie ahead for her now
She will speak, she will teach, she will help those who cannot help themselves
Ahead, the road is long
But soon we know she will be running like the wind
She knows it begins with a step"

My mother commemorated my accomplishment with this poem:

THE BRASS RING

Five years old,
Impatient to board the merry-go-round
She pushed past the benchlike seats,
The stationary horses,
Chose one that moved up and down.
The merry-go-round gathered momentum,
Music blared, excitement crossed her face,
She reached for the brass ring,
The merry-go-round slowed down.

She missed it. Maybe next time.
Throughout the years
She has ridden the merry-go-round many times
Trying to catch the brass ring.
Today her long distance call came.
She has something to share with me.
In autumn, when things come full circle,
The sign on her office will read
Dr. Marlene Charney Kushner
And underneath it an emblem:
The brass ring."

As I have written, the merry-go-round was one of the few rides that I could enjoy without experiencing severe motion sickness. However, since precise movement was beyond my capability, I never grasped that brass ring. With a great deal of effort, Nick purchased an authentic brass ring, which he affixed to the custom-framed poem that he and my mother presented to me.

With the fulfillment of my cherished dream, to be awarded my doctorate, came a number of related expectations. Having been subjected to misdiagnoses, my primary goal was to be as knowledgeable a clinician as possible. As my position did not require me to hold a doctorate, my employment continued much as before. I intended to establish a part-time private practice, and be free to determine which services would benefit my clients. I was also looking forward to having the time and opportunities to socialize. Therefore, I did not anticipate suffering a "postpartum" restlessness, and a sense of emptiness. After giving it much thought, and discussing my feelings with

Nick, we concluded that my reaction could be attributed to several sources:

1) a need to replenish myself

2) continuing fear of revealing my learning disabilities

3) my disabilities continued to evidence themselves to me. I would have to accept this, despite attaining the highest degree my profession awarded, and developing numerous compensatory measures. Of course, I consciously understood that this would be the case. Nevertheless, each time my symptoms expressed themselves, I feared that my degree would lead to expectations that I could not fulfill. Unless I knew everything about my field and never erred, my professional interventions would fall far short of acceptable. Nick encouraged me to hang my diploma, purchase personalized stationery, and refer to myself as "Doctor," when the occasion called for it. However, I would only indicate my new title when it was required.

Chapter 26

After a fairly short "recovery period", I began to explore how I could best put my training and talent to use. However, that exploration would have to be put on indefinite hold. It became difficult to remain at work for the full day, due to the increasing pain in my knee. John Peterson, a high-level administrator, told me that no one would believe my injury, as I wore flats rather than sneakers to work. In fact, the flats were more comfortable, as they were lighter and easier to slip off. My explanation was not accepted. I was shocked and devastated for two reasons. The first was that I highly valued my reputation as an honest person. The second was that this disbelief could have professional as well as personal ramifications. In fact, John, who was not a clinician, was skeptical of providing accommodations for students with learning disorders. Previously, he had shared personal experiences that might explain this disbelief. However, I decided that suggesting a relationship between the past and current perspectives to him would not be appropriate or beneficial.

The second auto accident greatly heightened my anxiety. Not only did I have recurrent flashbacks to the first accident, trauma from the second accident was now added to it. My fears and physical limitations were an enormous setback. As I wrote earlier, my vision had been slowly improving since the first accident. I had previously figured out the easiest routes and times of day for local travel, and was working up my courage to get behind the wheel again. Of course, I was out of practice, not having driven for a year. However, confronted with re-experiencing my visual impairment, I had to again consider whether it was safe to drive. Apart from the concern for myself, I believed it was unethical for me to drive if my visual limitations might result in an accident and injury to another person. However, I also worried that an emergency might arise, and I would be helpless to act. In fact, one did. One evening, Nick began to experience increasingly intense stomach pain. We called our physician, who told us to go to the emergency room. Unable to find anyone to do the driving, we decided that of the two of us, we were safer with Nick operating the truck. We did make it to the emergency room, mercifully a short distance away, where Nick was admitted with diverticulitis. I was devastated that I was unable to spare him the worsening of his symptoms.

The consideration to voluntarily give up driving was a deeply conflicted and painful one. On the one hand, it would be a great relief. On the other, it meant forgoing an independence that I had put forth a tremendous struggle to maintain for over three decades. Additionally, my husband would have to assume all responsibility for transportation. I felt unable to be the wife and helpmate Nick deserved; once again I felt like a powerless failure. I decided to allow myself a year before making the final determination as to whether I felt capable of driving. I had just purchased a new car. Seeing it every day as I walked to the train was a painful reminder of my condition. In that year, I underwent many tests and treatments. However, no one was able to provide me with any diagnosis or effective treatment for my visual disturbance. Ultimately, I was referred to an out-of-state expert, who conducted an exhaustive ophthalmic analysis. The results indicated significant, numerous visual deficits that had not been detected on earlier, less sophisticated instruments. Upon reading that report, I finally understood why I experienced severe anxiety each time I got behind the wheel. It was determined that it would be unsafe and unwise for me to continue driving.

I was physically and emotionally exhausted from dealing with all of my demanding obligations. Many of these requirements were made more onerous by the need I felt to disguise deficits I would evidence, unless I stayed continually on guard. In reflecting on how I could go forward, I determined that it would be necessary, although very personally threatening, to disclose that I had a number of learning disabilities. I began by sharing this information with the Director of the Center, Vic,who was very supportive. Being more confident about revealing myself, I decided to disclose this information to a colleague, Beau, with whom I worked very closely. I was shocked by his hostile response, which was that there had been no indication that I had any learning disabilities. Therefore, he did not believe what I had disclosed. My colleague would only consider the information valid if I provided documentation to him! Initially, I was shocked that I had temporarily "passed", but this was of little comfort. My colleague's reaction was not the one I had, with dread, expected. Ironically, I was accused of being dishonest by falsely claiming I had disabilities. In fact, my fear was that I would be accused of dishonesty by concealing my disabilities. I had imagined that any explanation regarding my disabilities and request for accommodations would be met with anger and disappointment. My preciously guarded image of myself as an honest person, and claim to be accepted as one, could legitimately be disputed. I would face humiliation, and my already poor self-image and confidence would further plummet. At some point, I would be disciplined for poor performance and terminated. I was overwhelmed by shame, guilt, fear, and anger.

My colleague concluded his statement of disbelief by offering me what he considered to be valuable advice. He said, "Regardless of whether or not what you told me is true, your disclosure would be a disservice to the students." He expressed his belief that their confidence in me would suffer as a result. I reflected on what he had said, and decided to trust my judgment.

Revealing that I experienced challenges, similar to the ones my students were contending with, proved to be very helpful to me and, more importantly, to them. I no longer had to emotionally look over my shoulder, and could breathe a sigh of relief. My focus did not have to be divided. I could be completely directed to what each student was sharing and needed. My self-disclosure was also beneficial to developing a rapport with the students. It bridged whatever differences (age, ethnicity, educational level, etc.) existed. I found that after a very short time, students shed whatever preconceived concerns they may have had about me, and were more likely to adopt my suggestions. Although their goals differed from mine, I represented the possibility that given the support, resources and opportunities, an individual with learning difficulties could succeed. Their accomplishments might be even more meaningful because of challenges courageously accepted and met.

Unfortunately, the satisfaction and joy I experienced in working with students was tempered by knee pain. Even the short walk to and from work was becoming very difficult. By the time I arrived home, I could do no more than collapse on the couch until dinner, and then go to bed. A surgical debridement did not reduce my pain, and it was determined I needed a knee replacement. The surgery went very well and I was expected to make a rapid recovery. However, my orthopedist used surgical glue to close my incision rather than staples. I developed a severe allergic reaction to it. In order to prevent an infection, I was given an antibiotic. Despite the medication, however, I developed clostridium difficile colitis (Cdif), a very severe infection, and had to be hospitalized. Therefore, I was unable to do physical therapy to strengthen my new knee. Once I was home, anxiety rapidly increased. I was concerned about how my inability to do anything but recuperate was impacting my employment and my relationship with my husband. Therefore, when Nick was invited to a cousin's home for Thanksgiving, I urged him to go, and assured him that I would rest and be fine. However, some hours after he left, I lifted myself off of the couch, and began walking to the bathroom. Suddenly, I was paralyzed with very severe pain, and could not move.

Fortunately, he was due home shortly. When Nick arrived, he immediately called for an ambulance. The paramedics could not get the stretcher up my narrow staircase, so I had to navigate myself down the flight of steps. Arriving at the hospital, I was examined and administered tests. I was diagnosed with a spinal lumbar herniation and needed a spinal fusion. That was followed by a very painful inpatient rehabilitation. It would be three months before I could return to work. I was extremely concerned about how my students were progressing without my support. On my first day back at the Center, my desk was piled high with students' folders. As the only psychologist in my department, my work had significantly accumulated. Nevertheless, I was thrilled to be useful once again, and to be needed.

I was overwhelmed, but so happy to be working with all of my students. However, I continued to experience significant pain from my left thigh to my knee. I made an appointment with Dr. Richard Balderson, who had performed the spinal surgery. After an examination and testing, he concluded that the pain was due to scar tissue, which had developed from the procedure. Therefore, it would be pointless to do further surgery, as the scar tissue would recur. He suggested physical therapy. I followed up on the referral, but my pain continued as before.

Chapter 27

Shortly after I returned to work, an additional responsibility was thrust upon Nick and me. My mother began re-experiencing the severe anxiety she had after my father's death. Losses of friends in her Senior Center classes exceeded her abilities to cope. The aide that we had previously hired when dad was ill was unavailable, so she recommended a co-worker. Unfortunately, after about six months and considerable expense, my mother's condition continued to deteriorate. We had been advised that it was best to allow an older person to remain in familiar surroundings. However, we concluded that mom's needs should be monitored by those closest to her. Once the decision was made, we had to wade through thirty years of papers and memorabilia, restore her apartment to its original condition, and pack or dispose of furniture and household goods. Each weekend, Nick and I made the three-hour trip, and accomplished as much as possible. We hoped that once mom was living with us, she would enjoy outings we would plan. In order to facilitate her transportation, we purchased an Explorer. It was fitted, so my mother could have easy access and it would accommodate a wheelchair.

About half way through our preparations to relocate mom, she awoke in terrible pain and was rushed to the emergency room. After a number of tests, it was determined that she had severe osteoporosis and spinal fractures. We were in shock, as she had few symptoms prior to the hospitalization. Mom was transferred to a local nursing home for rehabilitation. We would visit with her, and then prepare her apartment for the move, before making the trip homeward. Needless to say, we were beyond exhaustion. Finally, we were able to have mom move into our house.

Understanding that the steps would prove difficult for her, we suggested that a hospital bed be placed on the first floor. However, she preferred the second-floor bedroom. In fact, a visiting nurse told us that it would be therapeutic for my mother to climb the steps daily. Mom resisted. "Marl, you don't understand. It is too painful." As Nick and I both had to work, we interviewed a number of agencies for an aide. Fortunately, my mother, at age 85, had the foresight to maintain her finances and health. This enabled her to purchase long-term care insurance. While this would not cover all costs, it was of tremendous assistance. We initially preferred an aide who worked on an hourly basis. That way, we could maintain a degree of privacy at night.

Shortly after my mother arrived, she suffered another fracture, and was rushed to the hospital. Afraid to be alone in the hospital room, she insisted aides sit by her bedside, day and night. Given that hospitals recommend that a patient be accompanied by a family member or close friend, her request seemed to have merit. Unfortunately, my mother developed a mild case of pneumonia while in the hospital. When I paid my visit, the aide was sleeping, and my mother's I.V. was empty! We knew that changes had to be made. Mom recovered and was sent to a nursing home for rehabilitation. We used that time to research resources to meet mom's emotional requirements, before she returned to our home.

I spent a great deal of time convincing the staff of a geriatric counseling program that my mother would be a suitable candidate. They were concerned that her lack of mobility would prevent her from participating in the program. Once they had agreed to admit her, I began to have concerns. Mom was in a room by herself, with no television or radio. The rationale was to discourage patients from remaining in their rooms. However, I did not know whether she would be able to emotionally sustain herself under those arrangements. Another concern was the condition of the other patients. I had asked whether the behaviors of the other residents were aggressive, and was told that they were not. However, disorientation and memory deficits made some of their actions and conversations seem bizarre. Most of them were mobile, and had free time. I observed them wandering into my mother's room, where she was a captive audience. I was beginning to fear that this program would intensify her anxiety. As I was struggling with the pain of her condition and her environment, other issues arose which worsened the situation. The first was that mom suffered another fracture, this time while lying in bed. She was in agony, and moaned continuously during my visits. She then developed her second bout of pneumonia. Visits were torturous. I repeatedly checked with the medical staff, who assured me that she was receiving the maximum dose of pain medication her age would allow. That amount was not sufficient to manage her pain.

Further exacerbating the situation were the restrictions imposed upon me, and therefore on Nick, by my employment. I could only visit my mother after office hours, or on weekends. By the time I took the bus and train to the hospital after work, she was experiencing disorientation and delusions. Mom was in agony, waiting for her final medication before bedtime. It was also unsafe for a woman to be traveling alone in the city during evening hours. I was torn with guilt, and unsure if I should risk my position and well-being to spend more time with mom. I feared she would not be able to survive her conditions. I also weighed my duty to her against the potential costs to my husband. No matter what or how much I did for them, it seemed inadequate in the face of their legitimate, yet conflicting needs.

The situation was resolved, but not in the way that I anticipated. One night, mom called for assistance, and was unable to wait for the response. She attempted to climb out of bed, forgetting that she was attached by devices on her legs to prevent blood clots. Mom fell, and was rushed to the emergency room. Her pleas to call her daughter were ignored. Amazingly, she suffered no fractures. After she healed, to the extent that she could be transported, we were told that she was not a suitable candidate for the program, due to her physical limitations. Mom arrived at a nursing home badly bruised, and had thrush. She was also missing several teeth and her dentures. We contacted several attorneys for redress. We were told that, given the legal protections afforded by hospitals, and the limited financial reimbursement when an older person is injured, it was not a case worth taking. I was furious and deeply depressed, given the little value placed on my mother's wellbeing and life. However, I knew we had exhausted every resource and needed to move on.

There was a brief positive period during this time. My mother was placed in a room with a compatible roommate. She told us that she preferred to remain there rather than return to our home. Unfortunately, her roommate had to be moved to a different room. We were unable to find another suitable resident, so mom decided to return to our care.

With experience, we sadly understood that we would have to look for live-in help. We had repeatedly dealt with aides that arrived late or not at all. When that occurred, my mother became very anxious. Nick would then cancel or postpone client appointments. I was worried not only about what this would do to his business, but to his health and our relationship. Another benefit of a live-in aide was that it was less expensive than paying an hourly wage. Nevertheless, the costs we incurred when we did manage to have a live-in aide were substantial. Most aides do not prefer this arrangement. They have families and/or other obligations that make this arrangement difficult for them. In addition, my mother's fear of being alone in her room presented an untenable arrangement for anyone. Given mom's emotional state and requirements, it was extremely difficult to obtain and maintain someone who would accept her conditions. Initially, the aide was given a bedroom on the second floor, where Nick and I also slept. There is one small bathroom on that floor. Issues relating to adequate facilities and privacy necessitated that we relocate in our home. Fortunately, shortly after moving into our house, I encouraged Nick to convert the attic into a "man cave" for him and his friends. We had a comfortable couch with a large-screen TV and sound system, as well as a bathroom, partial kitchen, and small sleeping area. Although I was very disappointed that this would not be the hideaway we had planned, it served a critically important function.

Chapter 28

I feared for Nick's health and our relationship, as living conditions were extremely stressful. Apart from all of the above, he completed the ongoing monumental paperwork required by the aides' agencies, as well as the errands for the entire household. We provided the aides with every convenience and comfort. We went as far as searching the local stores for products and produce from their homelands. We tried in every way to be attentive to the aides' situations. In addition to their work, all of the caretakers had undergone very difficult lives. They told us of unimaginable brutality experienced in their war-torn countries. Many aides were struggling with legal and financial barriers, in order to bring their children to our country. They also described horrendous conditions in the homes of other clients, and pitiable stories about their nursing home employment. As we were caring listeners, we spent many hours providing support and suggestions. Most were appreciative and considerate (although one aide attempted to leave our employ with an $1,800 phone bill).

Obtaining mom's morphine was especially difficult. Prescriptions had to be handed to Nick If a drugstore had a limited supply, which he accepted, the balance could not be filled. Finally, Nick was often told that the drugstore had the full amount prescribed, only to arrive there and find that this wasn't the case. We had to accomplish all of this while contending with our respective injuries, therapies, appointments and paperwork associated with two complex cases. Last, but certainly not least, we had obligations to our students and clients.

We understood, only too well, that my mother's emotional demands created an environment where it was difficult to function. Despite everyone's efforts, my mother was most unhappy. She found our suburban location frightening, and complained, "There aren't enough people on the street". As I previously wrote, the stairs proved to be a problem. Despite our encouragement and inducements, mom said it was too painful to navigate the steps. Furthermore, she was very reluctant to leave her room for any reason. This resulted in ongoing struggles. We had arranged for a weekly psychiatric appointment, and mom had many other doctor visits as well. Each time she had to leave her room, a tremendous battle ensued. Similarly, while the shower was handicapped-equipped, it represented a threat to my mother, and she resisted mightily. She had always been very considerate of others. However, her illness and attendant fears resulted in mom making unreasonable demands on the aides. For example, in hot weather, she was uncomfortable with air conditioning. The aides, many of whom were heavy-set, could not stay in a hot room for an entire day. Issues frequently arose, which my husband or I attempted to resolve.

On returning from an appointment to get flu and pneumonia shots, my mother complained that her pain had greatly worsened. Although nothing adverse had apparently occurred, we rushed her to the emergency room. The E.R. physician found that she had suffered additional fractures. Mom's gerontologist strongly recommended that she be permanently placed in a rehab/nursing facility, as it was no longer safe for her to be transported to a hospital or doctor. We arranged for the social worker who was seeing her weekly, at our house, to continue her visits in the nursing home. My mother's hearing was impaired, and, at times, the effects of the medication further affected her cognition, short term memory and coordination. For most of my life, I had looked to my mother for advice on every important matter. Rarely did I feel that she was wrong. In fact, once I began to study neuropsychology, I began referring to my parents as my external frontal lobes. They provided me with the role models, strategies and encouragement that I needed to be successful. As many adult children with aged parents will attest, mine was an exquisitely wrenching situation and decision. Nick and I explored a number of local facilities. We selected one that had a good reputation, and was near enough for us to visit weekly. We chose a room right next to the nursing station, and mom actually seemed happier there than with us. I had mixed feelings about that. An especially difficult requirement was determining whether to sign the Do Not Resuscitate form. The decision was made somewhat easier by my mother's living will and the explanation that CPR would break all of her ribs. Reluctantly, I did sign, although I knew it could be a death sentence. Enduring the painful decline of my mother, I frequently recalled bittersweet memories. I found it almost unimaginable for her to be experiencing this painful quality of life. On occasion, though, mom did amaze me. Her foresight in certain circumstances was still better than mine. For example, her suggestion to put a cup in a secure place rather than the precarious location I had chosen, avoided an accident. Much more important than that, was the enduring love that my mother expressed for Nick and me.

Chapter 29

Despite the challenges I was facing on the home front, I pursued any resource that could improve the services I offered to my students. For the second time, I applied to the APA's Disability Issues Committee (CDIP). I hoped that the doctorate would increase my desirability as a candidate. Leaving nothing to chance, I sent my material return receipt requested. My application was again rejected. However, as a member of the APA, I was entitled to attend their meeting, at my own expense. I would have the opportunity to speak about the importance of addressing issues impacting individuals with learning disabilities. Although exhausted, Nick and I drove to Washington D.C., and I attended the meeting. The majority of members had visible disabilities. In my opinion, they did not indicate by their responses (or lack thereof) any interest in being involved in my subject. At the conclusion of the meeting, I requested that the chairperson keep me abreast of the activities of the committee. However, that did not occur. Greatly disappointed, I was determined to submit a third application and sent the following letter to the Executive Director for Public Interest:

Dear Dr. Tomes,
I am applying for membership on the Committee for Disability Issues in Psychology. My entire professional life has been dedicated to the study of and interventions for individuals who have learning and attentional disabilities. Based on my extensive training, clinical work and personal experience, I believe that I have much to contribute to the CDIP. This is my third application, but the first time I am revealing that I have learning disabilities. Past experience facing discrimination in academia, despite maintaining very high standards in my coursework, without benefit of accommodations, had previously caused me to be reluctant to disclose this information. However, I am being forthright in this situation as individuals with disabilities are encouraged to apply. According to my research, to date there has been no psychologist with expertise about the LD /ADD population on the CDIP. Given our unique relationship with this population in regard to service delivery, I strongly believe it is our responsibility to represent them through this forum.
I appreciate your consideration in this matter.

—Dr. Marlene Koestenblatt

To my great disappointment, frustration and anger, I was not appointed. Furthermore, I received no response to my inquiry as to whether any psychologist representing the LD/ADD population had ever sat on or would be appointed to this Committee. I felt that continuing my membership in the APA would conflict with my personal and professional ethics, so I wrote a letter of resignation. Upon submitting the letter, I had the smallest of hopes that my letter might engender a consideration of their current position, or lack thereof, but such was not the case. Therefore, I wrote the following letter.

Dr. Norman Anderson
APA Chief Executive Officer
Dr. Robert Sternberg
APA President

Dear Drs. Anderson and Sternberg,
I congratulate you both on your appointments, and wish you well as you face the many and significant challenges your positions entail. Your achievements to date will stand you in good stead. After reading your recent articles, I was impressed by the importance you place on listening to your constituents and advocating the willingness to change. I therefore decided that you might find my reasons for terminating my membership with APA useful.

I joined APA as a student many years ago, and have maintained my membership until this year. About twenty years ago, in the midst of completing a graduate program in Clinical Psychology, I was diagnosed with learning disabilities, and, subsequently, an attention deficit disorder. I ultimately earned my M.A. degree and was granted an Ed. D, with a specialization in The Neuropsychology of Learning Disorders. I have worked in institutions of higher education for most of my professional life. Given my personal as well as professional experiences, I was very enthused to learn about the Committee for Disability Issues in Psychology, and applied when the Monitor announced an open position. I was told, after the selection period, that my material had been lost. I traveled to the meeting, at my own expense. I was permitted a very short time to express concern about my constituents. The committee members did not indicate much interest. I was told by the chairperson that I would be kept informed of the Committee's activities, but have not received any correspondence. My second application was rejected. In response to my insistent questioning, I was told that no one on the Committee represented the population of individuals with learning and attentional disabilities. Since my diagnosis, I have dedicated myself to acquiring the best education I could, to keeping myself abreast of the most current information, and to maintaining those professional associations that would enable me to engage in the best practices possible. I believe the American Psychological Association has the power and the resources, but not the intention, to research and better serve the population of those who are challenged with "invisible disabilities."

Sincerely,
Marlene Koestenblatt Ed.D

Once again, I received no response to my letter.

Chapter 30

Nick had just completed about a year of physical therapy, necessitated by our second accident, when he was injured in a third auto accident. He was returning from a visit with my mother. While stopped in a line of traffic, he was rear-ended with great force. Arriving home from work, I became aware that something significant had occurred when I saw our neighbor waiting for me at the train station. Realizing immediately that something had happened to Nick, I was initially paralyzed with fear. We got into her car, and I managed to ask what had happened. She told me that Nick had been taken to the emergency room of our local hospital. I could barely breathe. Tears streamed down my face as I reached my husband. He actually looked alright. However, I had been through his three surgeries, each preceded by seemingly normal conditions. I became completely hysterical, causing the hospital personnel to rush into his room. Nick wanted me to lie down in his hospital bed, but his suggestion slowly allowed me to gain control. He was released and we returned home, where the following day I faced workplace challenges.

As much as I enjoyed working with the students, professional differences negatively affected the work environment. Prior to the disclosure of my learning disabilities, my colleagues frequently commented about my impressive knowledge and skills. They expressed amazement at my ability to understand what my students were experiencing, and what they would need to progress. I believed that my disclosure would provide greater credibility about my perspectives and recommendations, but that did not occur. Therefore, I began to consider other employment alternatives. Nick had created a beautiful home office for me. However, both of us felt that it wasn't feasible for me to leave work and start a private practice at that time. Nick suggested that I start seeing a few students on the weekends. He believed that the practice would grow, and ultimately, I could resign from my employment. While that seemed to have merit, I was reluctant, for several reasons. I needed the weekends to recuperate from the prior week, and prepare for the week ahead. While I found working with the students very rewarding, it was also draining. The emotions that were evoked in me upon hearing their pain, and the discrimination they encountered, were painful, and sapped my energy. In addition, I had sacrificed virtually all of my free time to study, and now wanted to spend time with my husband, family and friends. All of the above reasons were valid. I could acknowledge them to myself, and share them with Nick. These reasons did not threaten to bring to consciousness my profound lack of confidence to practice without oversight. I was between the proverbial rock and a hard place. I did not want to continue in my present position, nor did I have the courage to begin a private practice. My dad told me that when he had to make a difficult decision, he listed the positives on one side of a paper, and the negatives on the other side. He then acted upon the side that had the most entries. I decided to use this approach. One reason to stay was the security of a salary and benefits. Another was that I no longer had the fear of being exposed. There were two reasons to leave. When there was a choice between supporting the university and a student(s), as an employee, I was expected to support the school. Another was the belief that my personal and professional experiences better equipped me to understand my students' needs than my colleagues did, some of whom were my superiors. My path was still unclear.

While Nick and I were discussing my employment options, something happened at work that left little choice about my future at the college. I had come across a file that a colleague was looking for and put it on her desk. Vic then accused me of initially placing it where I had found it. Not only was this untrue, but there was no reason for me to have done that. It occurred to me that if I was charged and reprimanded about such an innocent act, it might be the beginning of attempts to remove me from my position. Even worse, my professional reputation and credentials as a psychologist could be in jeopardy. Although the cost would be significant, I felt it necessary to seek other employment.

Chapter 31

After a few months, I was given a part time position at another university's Disability Center. I would be working with students who had learning and attentional disorders, head injuries, medical conditions that affect cognition, autism, Asperger's Syndrome and various psychological disorders. Gradually, hours were added to my week, until I had full-time status. I was very happy with that development. My work was satisfying, my salary increased commensurately with my hours, and benefits were now included in my compensation package.

My positive employment experience helped me deal with the final illness and death of my mother. I received a call from her nursing home, informing me that mom's heart was failing, and only palliative measures were possible. I arranged for hospice services at the residence, and Nick and I quickly arrived there. My mother was aware of and clear about everything, other than her terminal state. She continued to be in charge of the very few decisions she had to make. As we leaned over her bedside, we felt a great sadness, alternating with emotional disbelief. When my mother's death was announced, all the aides that cared for her lined up outside of her room to pay their respects. They told us, "She will be missed. She was a real lady." Nick and I were very touched, and knew mom would very much appreciate their sentiments. When I phoned my supervisor, Julie, with the news, she told me that I was entitled to a week off. However, there were no friends or family who were available to sit shiva (pay condolence calls). I did not want us to mourn alone. I felt that working with my students would be helpful, and my mother would approve. So, Nick and I tried to distract ourselves by continuing with our routines.

Despite all of the advantages of my position, issues again began to emerge. My department had a small staff, all of whom were in their twenties or early thirties. They were comfortable and proficient with technology, whereas my knowledge and skills in that area were limited. As time passed, word spread about what we were offering, and appointment numbers soared. In part, this was due to my empathic understanding of the students' experiences and needs. We did not have sufficient staff to serve our growing population. While Julie repeatedly requested additional personnel, these requests were refused. In my previous experience, institutions welcomed growing student populations, which provided more tuition dollars. Staff was then commensurately increased. I was initially puzzled by the current situation until I considered how the population of my particular students might be viewed. I was not given an explanation of decisions that were "beyond my pay grade." The plan to deal with our increasing numbers of students was to more strictly limit the time spent with each one. I found that approach intolerable. I believed that the additional time, during which I provided information, recommendations and support, was essential to students' success. Another obstacle for me was the greater dependence on technology to handle increased data. As my stress level increased, my tendency toward disorganized thought and expression became more evident. My awareness of this increased my stress, and I was caught in a vicious downward spiral. Julie was clearly losing patience with me whenever I had to provide her with verbal information. At one point, she said to me, "Listening to you makes me sick. I don't want others to be sickened by you!" All my education and experience seemed irrelevant. I was traumatized, devastated and completely demoralized. I reported this comment to an administrator, who met with the two of us. It was a case of "she said, she said." Of course, I had no proof, and nothing was done. While the challenges in my professional life were significant, I would soon have to deal with the overwhelming loss of my marriage.

Over the course of our respective injuries, illnesses, treatments and the resulting financial ramifications, Nick and I were progressively becoming estranged. The manifestations of my disorders, which Nick found charmingly quirky early in our relationship, began to irritate him. The proverbial "final straw" occurred one evening in October 2012. A staff member noticed a large circular mark on the underside of my arm, and said that I should be checked for lyme disease. I called Nick, who drove me to my physician. She too thought I had lyme disease, and gave me preventative medication. By the time we arrived home, I was in severe pain from a reaction to the shots, and laid down on the living room couch. Nick suddenly shouted that he was tired of seeing me on the couch, unwilling to help myself. He felt entitled to a life, and no longer loved me. I was shocked and devastated by his statement. With that, he left me and our dog to go to the shore house of a client. On his return, he told me that I could have the house, and he would take what I had in savings. Although I had invested a great deal of money, as well as work and love in the house, it would be infeasible for me to live there on my own. I did not know how to maintain and repair the house. Furthermore, Nick's prior descriptions about corrupt and incompetent contractors made me fearful of hiring them.

In addition, it was difficult to climb the stairs to the second floor or down to the basement, where there was no banister and the laundry room was located. Desperate, I suggested that I move to the attic, and we see each other briefly on weekends. Nick had no comment. I stayed there for six months, after which time it became clear that he no longer wanted to be with me. In tremendous emotional pain, I decided to adopt a cat for company. Nick drove me to a shelter, where I fell in love with my new daughter, Ballerina. "Tiptoe" was given her nickname because a congenital condition caused her to walk on her toes. She could not bend, but had no trouble walking, or "flying through the air with the greatest of ease." "Tippy" always knew when I needed to cuddle, and was my devoted companion for eleven years. Once I had a roommate, I searched for and rented an apartment.

In exchange for giving Nick time to accumulate money for a mortgage in his name, he agreed to assist me in moving. He would also provide transportation for my doctor appointments and grocery shopping. This was the extent of his obligation. However, Nick made himself available for all of my apartment repairs, and personally delivered gifts for me on every occasion. Nevertheless, he was often very impatient, as he was exhausted from working seven days a week. Of course, interacting with him under these conditions was excruciating. Furthermore, I began to be concerned that, depending on my lifespan, I could well run out of money before the end of my life.

I had taken a two-bedroom apartment, and used one bedroom as an office. It was my intention to begin a private practice. However, after moving in, I was given a large list of rules by the management. This precluded having an office, along with many other restrictions. In addition, former neighbors I thought of as friends did not contact me. My current neighbors seemed uninterested in meeting new acquaintances. I dreaded another move within a year. However, living there was a social, emotional and financial impossibility. I began to look for another apartment.

One night, in the midst of searching for a new home, I awoke with frightening symptoms. I could not swallow or breathe normally, and was unable to eat or drink. After I was rushed to the emergency room, it was determined that my left vocal cord was permanently paralyzed, cause unknown. Fortunately, I had adequate volume in my voice to be heard under normal circumstances. However, the quality of the sound, as well as the need to take frequent short breaths, impaired my vocalizations. Breathing therapy was recommended to improve my ability to communicate. The deficit resulted in a major impediment to my capability to work. I had been using voice to text equipment to compensate for my keyboarding/learning disorder. The speech impediment required a great deal more effort. It also resulted in textual errors. Finally, the disorder increased the time needed to complete a very heavy caseload of notes. To protect confidentiality, I used my lunch hour to remove all personal information from each student's notes. After work, I brought them home to complete. Additionally, a staff member who had assisted me with technology left, and the new person only provided minimal help. I was exhausted, and the pressure became more intense.

Chapter 32

While I was struggling with the realization that my job was in jeopardy, an unrelated and unexpected event resulted in my termination a few months later. Nick called to tell me that he was passing by my office at closing time, and offered me a ride. While traveling home, we were yet again rear-ended! Fearful of losing my job, and experiencing minor symptoms, I returned to work the following day. However, by that evening, I was beginning to feel ill and in pain. Nick took me to an urgent care facility, where the physician recommended that I go to the emergency room. He suspected I had suffered a concussion, as well as bruising to my spine and legs. Fearing the consequences of missing work, I assured myself I could function, and declined. Nevertheless, the following day I had a very painful headache, my imbalance was severe, and my grip was significantly affected. I called Julie at home to notify her as soon as possible about my condition. I left a message that I had been injured in an accident, would be out, and would contact her after seeing a physician. My appointment the next day with a neurologist confirmed a severe concussion. He said I should not work for at least several weeks, upon which I would have my next appointment. I had him fax the recommendation to Julie and called her at the office. As she did not answer, I left her a message. When Julie returned my call, she said, "You did not follow procedure by calling me at home, rather than at the office!" I explained, "I attempted to notify you as soon as possible. My symptoms were progressively incapacitating." I was told, "If you fail to come in, you will be fired!" Of course, I was unable to get to the office, much less work effectively, so I was terminated. There was also an attempt to deny me unemployment benefits, but I was found eligible.

For several months, I was on the waiting list for an outpatient rehabilitation program. During that time, I struggled to manage my household responsibilities. Finally, I was enrolled in a specialized concussion program at Bryn Mawr Rehabilitation Hospital. This entailed my traveling, by train, to the hospital. I needed a walker to get to the station. However, my balance was so impaired that I had a problem using it. The staff expressed concern about this, but I had no other option. No family members lived nearby, and everyone I knew worked during the day. The program began with patients and their caregivers seated in the waiting room. It was very painful for me to be unaccompanied. I reminded myself how fortunate I was, in comparison to the other patients, who had suffered more severe injuries. While my skills started to improve, the travel, therapy, and home exercises required a good deal of my time and energy. In addition, I had to deal with appointments and paperwork related to unemployment as well as the divorce. Finally, I had to prepare for moving, having begun arrangements prior to the accident. After seven months, the therapists told me that my skills had plateaued. I was released from the program with congratulations from the staff for what I had accomplished. I had been able to significantly reduce symptoms resulting from the concussion. Unfortunately, the pain in my spine and legs continued with little diminishment.

Chapter 33

I believed that the very painful process of divorce would be finalized within about a year. However, as I met with my attorney, and reviewed the paperwork, it became increasingly clear that my legal representation was not proceeding as it should. Despite the tension between us, I shared my misgivings with Nick. He agreed that there were issues that needed to be resolved. Ultimately, both of us engaged in an arbitration. I was awarded damages and engaged a new attorney.

I was relieved that I was found justified in pursuing my case, and awarded financial compensation. However, it was a pyrrhic victory. Alone in my apartment, I was overcome with anxiety, loneliness and sadness. I had lost almost everything at once. I doubted each significant choice I had made throughout my adulthood. My life was little more than an endless struggle, empty and frustrating. I did not value the enormous effort I had made to be better equipped to handle my life, and contribute to family, friends and my profession. The impending divorce was depriving me of more than the love and companionship of my husband. I no longer could identify myself as a wife. As I was not part of a couple, some of my former "friends" disappeared. Unable to maintain my house by myself, I had to leave the home I was invested in, loved, and considered a source of security. I now had to handle all major decisions and household responsibilities. Many of these tasks were exceedingly difficult, due to my prior injuries and multiple disabilities. Finally, the loss of my employment did not only have financial consequences. I no longer was actively working as a neuropsychologist. I therefore was deprived of another significant component of my life which gave it meaning: working with and for my students.

There were several factors that motivated me to continue taking action. The progressive depletion of my savings, my work ethic, and my sense of personal responsibility were always on my mind. Therefore, the government's requirement that I apply for a number of jobs per period to receive unemployment matched my own goals. Nevertheless, sending many cover letters and resumes that received no response was very painful and frightening. I knew I needed support, and was able to begin a therapeutic relationship with a dedicated psychiatrist. Unlike most of his peers, Dr. James Brady provided both "talk therapy" as well as medication. He prescribed many medications with no improvement in my depression or anxiety. Desperate, I begged him to prescribe Xanax, as it had previously been helpful. Reluctantly, after explaining all of the possible side effects, he agreed. Once more, I found it very helpful.

Chapter 34

About two years after my separation from Nick, I replied to an ad from a local psychologist, Dr. Hall. This opportunity presented itself around Christmas. I hoped that it was a harbinger of a good start for the upcoming year, and immediately responded. I was informed that he was interested in having a neuropsychologist join his staff. Excitedly, I scheduled an interview. To update my professional knowledge, I purchased a lengthy technical text which I read and absorbed in two days. That winter we had a number of ice storms, but I did not want to risk postponing my interview. With high hopes, I carefully walked to a nearby train, and enthusiastically arrived for my appointment. I naively sustained the outlook that a position was in reach thanks to a growing number of interviews. Dr. Brady repeatedly warned, "You are being used as a source of free instruction." I insisted, "You are wrong. I must demonstrate my knowledge and skill!" Unfortunately, over time, it became clear that my therapist's prediction was accurate. Confronting Dr. Hall, he continued to stall about hiring me. I wrote a letter calling him out, but it brought little satisfaction.

I continued to apply regularly for positions, but didn't expect to receive an offer. Nevertheless, I wanted to be prepared for any opportunity. I continued my membership in AHEAD, a professional organization for postsecondary disability service providers. I also was reading research on learning disabilities, and the growing body of material about attentional disorders. I continued to find neuroscience to be the most fascinating of subjects. This exploration expanded my clinical expertise, and the understanding of my own functioning. I knew that my learning disabilities included dyslexia, dyscalculia (miscalculations), and dysgraphia (poor handwriting), as well as issues with short-term working and spatial memory/reasoning. As I continued to learn about attentional disorders, it became clear that I possessed most of the characteristics attributed to this condition as well. I am restless, readily distractible, have difficulty paying attention, and organizing my thoughts, as well as my written expression. It is difficult for me to concentrate unless I am interested in the material. I am impulsive in thought and overcompensate for time management issues. My balance, as well as fine and gross motor coordination, are impaired. My visual processing focuses only on what is directly in front of me. This is very frustrating to experience, and difficult to explain. Let me give an example. Prior to our separation, Nick purchased a bicycle for me and placed it in our living room. He asked me to go into the room on a pretext, and waited for my response. There was none. My brain processed only what was directly in front of me. I did not "take in" the entire living room, which is ample but not enormous. This is why my refrigerator is arranged with similar items grouped together, so I can fairly easily find them. Visual clutter makes me anxious, which further impedes my performance. Once I understood that all of these deficits affected my functioning, my lack of trust in myself finally made sense. Reviewing this lengthy list in 2022, it may seem incredible that these manifestations were not seen as a syndrome, or misinterpreted/misdiagnosed.

As I wrote earlier, I, and many like me, continually asked ourselves, "WHAT IS WRONG WITH ME?" I have included this personal material, as well as the final chapter, to enlighten and encourage those of you who are still asking: "*What is wrong with me? What is possible for me to achieve? What legal protections are available? Where can I go for information and assistance?*"

Chapter 35

As I continued my independent study on the interactions between the environment and emotional/neurological functioning, I focused on my apartment. I arranged everything to be as organized as possible. As household management became easier and less stressful, I became aware of a new concern. I detected a strong odor of soiled laundry throughout the apartment, even after all the wash had been done. At first, I re-doubled my efforts to clean, but the odor grew more powerful. My research of probable causes led me to investigate whether mold was contaminating the air. I bought a mold detection kit and set it up. Soon after, I saw evidence of black mold. I brought this sample to the apartment manager. She authorized a professional search, which verified my findings. I had to leave almost immediately, could take very little with me and had to quickly decide where I would relocate.

Reviewing my options was very discouraging. Initially, I decided against moving back to my apartment once it had been decontaminated. Therefore, I needed a temporary place to stay while I looked for a longer-term residence. Living in my home offered one possibility. Prior to my current situation, Nick raised the subject of reconciliation. He had taken a full-time position as a technician for a realty company and was working at his own business on the weekends. Nick now had company-provided health insurance and more regular weekday hours. However, as unhappy as I had been living alone, I no longer identified myself as his wife. Restoring the trust I had in him seemed impossible. Nevertheless, our divorce had not been finalized and I was still enabling him to refinance the mortgage. I decided to return to my house until I was well and could find a new place to live. I called Nick, explained my situation, proposed that I sleep on the living room sofa, and he agreed to that arrangement.

I was relieved when he picked me up, and got my medications as well as whatever else I needed. I remained on the living room couch for many months, slowly recuperating from the exposure to mold. Our relationship was improving along with our communication. I understood that a childhood of financial insecurity made him anxious about mounting debt caused by our accident-related injuries. Nick had believed that our marriage could not be sustained with his schedule, which had him working almost around the clock. Sadly, I did not have the support or counsel of my psychiatrist about this or any other matter. Dr. Brady had become ill. Soon after he stopped his practice, my beloved therapist passed away. I then began an outpatient program for individuals suffering from elevated anxiety. This provided counseling and techniques for dealing with my emotions. It also enabled me to obtain various benzodiazepines. During this time, Nick and I spent a great deal of time discussing the issues that led to our separation. We agreed about changes we both needed to make. I understood that it was necessary to begin with small steps for the reconciliation to progress. It would be a lengthy and effortful process to once again trust Nick's feelings for me. When I was emotionally prepared for it, I moved from the living room to the guest room, which was across the hall from the master bedroom. Eventually, I moved back into our bedroom.

I had to re-adjust to being a wife, but also to a very different residence from the ones in which I had been living over the past three years. My large, century-old home, with four sets of stairs, required much more time and effort to stock, clean, organize and repair than a small one-bedroom apartment. Nick provided transportation for all errands and appointments. As he enjoys preparing meals and is excellent at it, he took on that responsibility, as well as that of maintaining our home. While Nick assisted with daily chores when necessary, his schedule was full. Unfortunately, additional tasks aggravated the pain in my back and legs. It limited my functioning, as well as affecting my sleep. Since surgery was no longer an option, I made an appointment with Dr. Valley, a physician whose specialty is pain management.

I was given spinal injections, which were effective, but the relief only lasted a few months. With great reluctance on my part, I was then prescribed opioids. Once the minimal dosage proved inadequate to keep my pain bearable, I asked for and received the maximum amount. After using opioids for about a year, the maximum dosage was no longer effective. I discussed this with Dr. Valley, and decided to have him implant a spinal device to reduce my pain. Without consulting him or any other physician, I then decided to stop using benzos, as well as opioids. En route to the scheduled surgery, we were rear-ended one block from the facility. An ambulance transported Nick and me to the nearest hospital. Initial assessments indicated we had suffered sprains and strains. I had symptoms of yet another concussion. Dr. Valley determined it was necessary to wait a month before rescheduling the procedure. I understood, but was frustrated, and in great pain. Finally, I was again on the way to my implantation, and praying that all would be well. The surgery was a success. After a short period of healing, my pain was significantly reduced. Each day, for about a half hour, I would have to put a small charging unit where the spinal implant had been placed. This was a minor inconvenience, a small price to pay for the relief of agonizing pain. It allowed me to resume my normal activities.

Chapter 36

It was now time to begin the process of discontinuing my use of benzodiazepines, as well as opioids. Naively, I did not consider myself addicted to either of these medications, as I had never increased dosages beyond what was prescribed. I also had no experience with any friends or family undergoing this process. Therefore, I greatly underestimated what I was going to experience. Surprisingly, withdrawing from opioids posed little problem. However, gradually withdrawing from benzos caused overwhelming anxiety. I understood that I needed guidance, but did not believe I needed to be hospitalized, or enrolled in an ongoing support program. After several frustrating attempts to obtain guidance, Dr. Valley reached out to me. He advised me to withdraw only from the opioids. Once that was achieved, I should gradually reduce my dosage of benzos until that process was completed. It took all of my dedication and determination, but I was successful and have never resumed either medication.

That accomplished, I again sought the services of a therapist to assist me in dealing with life unmedicated. Gratefully, I established a relationship with Dr. Marianne Martino. The pride I felt in my dual withdrawal was overshadowed by an ongoing anxiety so severe that I was literally gasping for breath. In conjunction with that, the palpitations of my heart made my body feel as though it was vibrating, and the sound of my heart beat roared in my ears. My tendency to be easily distracted became even more extreme. I was struggling to eat, and rapidly losing weight. Sleeping was also impacted, and I was exhausted. Initially, I felt a great shame in exhibiting my symptoms, and in discussing them with Dr. Martino. I believed that I had failed in therapy and felt hopeless. I was frustrated and disgusted with myself. How could I be so compromised, after being fortunate enough to have had excellent therapists throughout my adulthood? Given my thoughts and emotions, I did not feel I deserved to take a therapist's time. Nevertheless, I was conflicted. Should I discontinue therapy, the enormous effort that I and my therapists had devoted would have come to nothing. That would also be true of the support given to me by my family and friends. Last, but certainly not least, it would end my lifelong goal of using my education and experience to guide others who hadn't had my opportunities. Therefore, I continued the most difficult psychotherapeutic work I had ever undertaken. Dr. Martino enabled me to understand and accept that to mitigate the impact of multiple traumas over many years would require my sustained efforts.

In order to continue the significant progress I had made, a new approach was needed. I sought out and began Cognitive Behavioral Therapy (CBT) with Dr. Sophie Longwill. This was an entirely different approach from the decades that I had undergone psychoanalytically based psychotherapy. The former approach differed in a number of ways from CBT. The focus had been on re-experiencing my past through projecting perspectives about significant people in my life onto my therapist. My dreams and thoughts were interpreted through a Freudian theoretical framework. My homework was to apply what I had learned in my sessions to understanding myself. The anticipated time frame was unlimited.

In contrast, the emphasis on CBT is on challenging present-day illogical, hurtful and unproductive thoughts that were impacting my emotions, bodily reactions and behaviors. I was given books to read and assignments with deadlines to complete. One very important series of assignments had me constructing personal daily and weekly schedules. Prior to that time in my life, the external structures imposed by academia and employment dictated how my days would be spent. While I experienced ongoing pressure to accomplish everything required of me in a timely way, the external structures were also helpful. They provided boundaries. My CBT therapy had me designing personal calendars, so that I could fulfill the duties of my adulthood and include leisure activities. I used up a great deal of time, effort, print cartridges and paper before I was satisfied with my products. As the ways in which I spent my time evolved, my calendars were updated to changing circumstances.

During this period, I was also extremely fortunate to have found a compassionate and dedicated psychiatrist. Dr. Martijn Figee prescribed a low-dose medication that was helpful when many, many others had failed. After I explained my current functioning to him, he very aptly coined the phrase "struggling successfully." That is to say,

I now was able to "redirect" painful reflections, and enjoy everything the present offered me.

I have come to terms with very painful and difficult decisions I had to make. For many years I wondered whether Steve and I should have continued trying to strengthen our marriage and family. I now believe that we were basically incompatible. Even had we known about my disabilities, I think Steve would have found it very difficult to accept my deficits and career choices, although he would have attempted to do so. It requires a great deal of understanding, patience and a sense of humor to deal with the many manifestations of my disorders. Nick has to deal with my struggle for self-acceptance as well. In support of our decision to divorce, Steve and Carolyn were happily married for many years. Erik has a strong bond with Carolyn and their extended family, for which I am very grateful. I, too, have a loving partner in my marriage. We have a wonderful relationship with our son, Erik, and with Meg, our terrific daughter-in-law. Some years ago Erik observed that his parents' differences are so great that it is remarkable we ever married! He added that he is the luckiest person he knows, having four great parents.

I am indeed a late bloomer. At this stage of life, I have the time and confidence to complete my memoir, a project I have been invested in throughout my adulthood. I resumed my private practice. I no longer have to choose between leisure activities and my professional life. I have a wide circle of friends with whom to share healthy activities. I very much enjoy volunteering as a friend for the Haverford Township Free Library. Now that my present is enriched, I have begun to explore my past. Membership in

Ancestry has made this search inexpensive and relatively easy. I am curious about my genetic and familial heritage. It could be wonderful to meet with my paternal family members. However, as my expectations are realistic, I am not concerned about rejection or what I might learn.

APPENDIX

Information and Resources

Chapter 1

I am offering just enough information to whet the appetites of those of you who have an interest in neuroscience, psychology, law and the way they interact in higher education. I will begin with an abbreviated history of protective legislation that encouraged and made it possible for the growing population of students with disabilities to enter and graduate from postsecondary institutions.

Section 504 of the Rehabilitation Act of 1973 is a civil rights law that prohibits discrimination on the basis of disability at all operations of colleges, systems of vocational education, universities or other postsecondary institutions, public systems of higher education, local educational agencies, or other school systems that receive federal funding.

Public Law 94.142, otherwise known as The Individuals with Disabilities Act (IDEA), was passed in 1975. It guarantees a free, appropriate public education to each child with a disability.

American with Disabilities Act of 1990 (ADA) defines a disability as "A physical or mental impairment that substantially limits one or more of the major life activities, a record of such impairment or being regarded as having such an impairment."

The ADA defines a qualified individual with a disability as "One who meets the academic and technical standards requisite for admission or participation in the institution's educational program or activities." Otherwise stated, a person with a disability is qualified if, with or without accommodation, the individual meets the same eligibility requirements, performance levels and behavioral standards set for everyone else.

Under the ADA, a postsecondary accommodation must be considered reasonable in order to be granted. There are four categories of accommodations that are not considered reasonable:

The accommodation cannot present a direct threat to the safety or health of other individuals.

The accommodation cannot result in a significant modification to an essential curricular component. The accommodation cannot result in an excessive administrative or financial burden.

The accommodation cannot change the way services are provided.

Americans with Disabilities Amendments of 2008 (ADAA) retains the ADA definitions but broadens the scope of coverage. It has the effect of making it easier to prove an impairment is a disability.

The IDEA and ADAA exist to protect the rights of disabled individuals. However, there is a significant distinction between the goals of the two. The intent of the IDEA is to promote success in children from K-12, while the objective of the ADAA is to ensure access for postsecondary students.

In addition to meeting the criteria set forth by either the IDEA or ADAA, an accommodation request must be based on the association between the barrier to learning or performance, and the individual's disability. In other words, a student with a disability may not require accommodation to achieve acceptable performance-to meet established standards.

Legislation to provide for the needs and protect the interests of students with special needs is an ongoing process. U.S. Senators Bob Casey (D-PA), Bill Cassidy (R-LA), Maggie Hassan (D-NH) and Todd Young (R-IN) introduced the Respond, Innovate, Succeed and Empower (RISE Act) to help ease the transition from high school to college for students with disabilities. The legislation would amend the 1965 passage of the Higher Education Act (HEA). RISE clarifies that students with previous documentation of a disability would be able to continue using that documentation as proof when they transition to higher education. This would help ensure that students who receive accommodations because of a disability do not need to spend time and money to go through unnecessary new diagnostic testing. The RISE Act would also make school policies and data more transparent for students and families, so they can make informed decisions on the college that best fits their needs. Finally, the legislation would provide additional support for technical assistance to colleges and universities, to better serve students with disabilities. The RISE Act has passed in the House of Representatives and is up for consideration in the Senate as of the writing of this book.

RISE is an example of legislation which reflects a paradigm shift. The primary source of information about a student's need for accommodation would be the interactive process. This refers to the discussion between the student and the staff responsible for determining accommodations. Twenty-four organizations that provide support and/or information to individuals with disabilities endorse this legislation. AHEAD, the organization of which I am a member, is among them. I agree with their position, which is general acceptance of the legislation, with certain caveats. I offer my professional experience as illustrative.

Chapter 2

The majority of students I served had been enrolled in the public school system. As I anticipated, students living in low-income communities often, unfortunately, received a poorer education than their more affluent peers. Those that had learning disabilities and attentional disorders were, therefore, less likely to be correctly identified, diagnosed, remediated and provided appropriate services and accommodations. There were several reasons for this. Evaluation professionals often were in short supply. In addition, if the assessment indicated that a student was eligible for accommodations and services, the school could incur a significant expense. In my experience, this outcome tended to be avoided, if possible. If a student was determined to have special needs, ongoing assessments were generally mandated throughout the youngster's enrollment. However, many of the students I worked with had very cursory examinations beyond the initial evaluation. Private assessments were often extremely expensive and beyond the budgetary constraints of most parents. I found myself in the frustrating and painful position of being unable to provide accommodations that were essential to the academic viability, much less the success, of a student. This deprivation often had several potentially life-altering consequences. Without the information about what was necessary for these students to succeed academically, they were significantly less likely to consider themselves capable of benefiting from post-secondary training or education. If they did apply and were accepted, they did not have the experience or knowledge to prepare for and deal with the more rigorous and independent performance standards of higher education. Vitally important self-advocacy skills had not been developed. Finally, they did not have the documentation required to be eligible for post-secondary services. Frequently, these students exhausted their financial aid by retaking first level courses. On some occasions, parents would sacrifice what little savings they had to allow their child to continue his/her studies, but to no avail.

In contrast, my students who lived in affluent communities were often enrolled in highly competitive school districts, where there was significant pressure to excel. The curriculum was enriched and supported by plentiful resources. However, misinformation or lack of information about learning disorders, coupled with fear of discrimination and stigma, resulted in the perspective that only those who had (or appeared to have) no learning differences would succeed in school and beyond. This was true of parents, as well as school personnel. In my experience, therefore, a number of these students either were not evaluated, or were assessed as youngsters and parents did not disclose the results of testing to the school or the student. Unfortunately, some of these students were unable to develop their potential, while others experienced success but at great personal cost. I recall one dedicated student coming to me who was having significant difficulty in all his courses. After we spoke, I encouraged him to reveal this struggle to his parents. He returned with very dated documentation, and said that his parents had hidden this material in their safe! The student was very confused, upset and angry. However, updated testing produced needed documentation. He was then provided with services, and his grades began to improve. Of course, not every intervention led to success.

Finally, youngsters are not well served when their grades are inflated. There are two common reasons for this. The first results when parents pressure faculty to increase the grade on a student's test or assignment to what mom and dad feel is deserved or needed to achieve a future accomplishment. The college admission scandal, where parents had their children's records falsified to gain them admission to prestigious universities, is an extreme case in point. When the falsification involves requesting accommodations for a non-existent disability, there are often ramifications that extend beyond the individual case. When the falsification becomes known, it tends to give weight to the skepticism that students with "invisible disabilities" encounter.

The second scenario results when a student is promoted from year to year with little regard for what has been learned. When students have consistently been given grades that do not accurately reflect their performance, they are unprepared for a more accurate assessment of their work. This often has emotional as well as academic consequences. Students who had this experience came to me and expected to be told that their instructors were unreasonable in their evaluations. I took great care to explain why their tests or assignments were fairly evaluated.

In contrast to the above scenarios, I had occasion to visit private schools where the curriculum was designed to meet the instructional needs of the LD/ADHD students. The material was presented innovatively and creatively. The students appeared very engaged and demonstrated a substantive grasp of the concepts. The diagnostic evaluations provided by these schools were generally current, and covered all areas of strengths and weaknesses. Unfortunately, apart from any scholarships offered, the tuition is generally beyond the means of most families.

RISE is being proposed to ameliorate the issues that many of my students encountered. The legislation coincides with the emerging paradigm of elevating students' reports of their learning needs as primary in determining accommodations. It is therefore very important for students to understand and communicate their learning and accommodation profiles, as well as to be advocates for themselves. As I previously wrote, many students are not offered training in self-advocacy until they are in college. Not every post-secondary institution offers this instruction. Furthermore, many students are uninterested or reluctant to advocate for themselves. The disability specialists' ability to understand the documentation provided, as well as to interpret the significance of their students' communications and behaviors, is of equal importance. Fortunately, there are currently a growing number of programs to prepare post-secondary students to become disability specialists. (When I began working with disabled college and graduate students, the field was newly emerging, with all that implies). As I noted above, there is a caveat to the RISE mandate. When documentation is non-existent, very dated or limited, and/or the student is unprepared to communicate instructional needs, additional steps may be required. AHEAD is currently obtaining feedback on this matter and will provide guidance when available.

<u>Chapter 3</u>

The passage of protective legislation, and developments in clinical research and practices, as well as in educational pedagogy, have significantly increased the possibilities and options for students with special needs to apply and be admitted to institutions of higher education. Concurrently, progress in these domains support the growing awareness and acceptance by these students, as well as by educational professionals and others who provide them services, that students previously considered incapable of benefiting from higher education are, in fact, "college material."

The United States Department of Education National Center for Statistics reported that in 2015- 2016, 19% of undergraduates self-identified as being disabled. The most commonly reported type of disability among undergraduates in private 4 year U.S. colleges were specific learning disabilities, with 36% of the disabled population reporting that condition. The second most commonly reported disability was ADHD, with 26% of the population of students with disabilities disclosing that syndrome. The actual number was probably 2 or 3 times higher, as nearly ⅔ of students who received accommodations in high school did not disclose their disability in college. As my academic history and the disclosures of others attest, there were students with "invisible disabilities" enrolled in colleges and universities prior to tabulating statistics, and well before that. The posthumous "diagnoses" of some of the most creative and brilliant contributors to society suggest that such students existed centuries ago.

The growing number of students with special needs in higher education are expecting and, in some instances, demanding to be seen, heard and respected. Of course, this stems from an emerging self-respect and self-confidence. When I was composing my dissertation in 1998, I was informed by my advisor that the appropriate terminology for such students was "individuals with a disability." This communicated that a disability was only one component of an individual. "There is much more to me than my difference, my disability. Please see the whole of me and don't be dismissive," might be a way to capture this sentiment. In contrast, I currently have been reading that individuals with special needs are beginning to prefer being described as "disabled persons", the disability being understood as an essential defining attribute. "I am proud of the entirety of my being".

This issue of self-definition brings to my mind a related topic. Individuals like myself who have "invisible disabilities" have the option "to pass" as neurotypical, at least initially. However, both anonymity as well as self-disclosure may impose steep costs and result in finding oneself between the proverbial "rock and a hard place." If we acknowledge our particular needs, which can, in itself, be painful and anxiety-provoking, we may either be disbelieved or determined to be incapable. Should we initially not disclose our condition, and perform without needed accommodations, we might be seen as incapable and/or ultimately untrustworthy. Finally, even when the additional time and effort to compensate result in successful performance, there are often significant costs to bear. As I have previously stated, the label of "learning disabled" resulted in my being denied enrollment to an institution that I was otherwise qualified to attend. In addition to encountering discrimination, I experienced ongoing fear of exposure, anger when hiding this "shameful" condition, sacrifice of time with family and friends, and exhaustion by constantly trying to "keep up." Despite often being the least costly conditions to accommodate, removing barriers for students with "invisible disabilities" continues to raise the issue of compromised academic standards, more so than with other conditions.

Given the complexity of these matters, it is not surprising that students and families I have worked with invariably raise the question of whether or not to disclose their disability and need for accommodation when beginning a new venture. The advancements I discussed earlier have significantly improved the quality of life for a student such as I was, decades ago. Unfortunately, however, it may still be a difficult decision to make, as ignorance and discrimination continue to be realities. I do not believe there is one right answer as each student's particular circumstance is unique. Rather, I suggest that there are certain issues that should be considered before making a decision. Whenever possible, I have found it helpful to reflect on how experiences similar to the one under consideration were handled. What was necessary for a successful outcome? I firmly believe in the importance and appropriateness of accommodations when indicated. However, the ability to meet or exceed performance standards in the essential duties of a course, program or career is crucial. It is very important to find out if success in areas of deficit is possible by exerting additional time/effort, using assistive technology or strategies, etc. What are the supports and resources? I advise researching to determine one's comfort level and ability to have needs met in the new environment.

I will provide a personal example to illustrate these suggestions. As I wrote earlier, I had become interested in the discipline of psychology as a youngster, when my mother described her courses in adult education. Before beginning college, I reviewed the courses required to obtain a Bachelor of Arts degree. Eight sample semesters were suggested, five courses in each. I determined that the maximum number of courses I could successfully handle would be four. Most probably, I would have to take one course after my final semester, delaying graduation. I accepted that. I also knew that taking courses each summer session would be necessary. In reviewing the courses needed to major in psychology, I anticipated that statistics (or "sadistics" as I renamed this course), would be very difficult for me. Considerably more time would be needed for me to master this course than was generally suggested. I decided to take statistics over the summer, whenever offered, so I could devote all my time to mastering it. I knew that summer courses were shortened and therefore I would have to process the information more quickly than in the fall, but decided that was the better of the two options. As I wrote earlier, the stress of undergraduate statistics was intensified when our professor discussed the classes' midterm grades. He announced that everyone had failed so he destroyed all our tests. The final would determine my grade for the course. With Steve's help, I was successful!

Being enrolled in statistics taught me an additional lesson. After taking the final, all the students gathered outside the classroom to discuss each question. We had been given a paper with test items and one question was on the blackboard, the score of which constituted fifty percent of our grade. When we began to discuss that item, one student became hysterical. She had been so stressed that she failed to see the question. She immediately re-entered the classroom but the professor adamantly refused to consider any option to retake the item. I vicariously experienced academic trauma. Going forward, whenever I took an exam, I checked everywhere additional questions could appear ! I continued to struggle with statistics throughout my master's and doctoral programs, as I was being prepared to conduct research and evaluate the studies of others. However, I applied a similar approach with each statistics course and achieved success.

In contrast to my success with statistics, I, along with my professors, continued to be perplexed by my issues with written expression. We could not understand why, despite everyone's efforts, my work was very disorganized. I had no difficulty with the mechanics or content of the material and could only see the problem after it had been commented upon and graded. Without a depth of understanding about how I processed information, certain of my grades were impacted by my learning differences. However, I devoted myself to my studies, to the exclusion of all activities other than those that were essential. With that considerable sacrifice, I was able to make the Dean's List every semester as an undergraduate.

I hope that readers might benefit from my experiences as a student. More importantly, investigate the resources that were not available to me throughout most of my studies. Understand the material in any evaluations you have been given. If you have not been previously assessed, or if your testing is dated and does not provide information useful for current performance, seek a current evaluation if possible. This information will be helpful in advocating for yourself. As I previously wrote, you may benefit from some instruction and support in self advocacy as it is uncomfortable for many students who have had no experience and/or preparation for it. It certainly was for me! Sharing yourself in a group of other students who have similar challenges to yours can provide some useful suggestions and also be supportive. In summary, take advantage of the resources that are here for you so that you can experience good health, enjoyable activities and meaningful relationships, as well as succeed academically! The previous recommendations can be very beneficial in the process of developing a healthy self-understanding.

This benefit to an individual can ultimately lead to positive cultural re-definitions. More flexible academic and vocational choices that are aligned with an individual's abilities and interests would be promoted. Current information about the required education, training, skills and opportunities of countless possible careers should be included in high school curriculum, but often are not. As I stated earlier, knowledge about one's interests and strengths, as well as vulnerabilities, are very useful when making academic, as well as vocational decisions. While this knowledge is important for all students, it is particularly so for those with special needs, due to additional considerations. Therefore, internships at the high school and college level are especially valuable. They allow all students to experience the match between one's abilities and the requirements of a position. Internships also enable special needs students to learn what accommodations might be allowed and helpful in an employment setting. In this way, they serve another purpose. The information may overcome reluctance on the part of a student or his/her professor to consider a classroom accommodation, based on the unproven assumption that it would be unavailable when the student is employed.

Chapter 4

Due to my training in neuropsychology, my personal and professional experiences, and my fascination with neuroscience, I continually access current as well as historical literature in my field. As such, my knowledge of both learning disabilities and attentional disorders continues to grow. I learned that the behavioral manifestations of attentional deficits were noted centuries ago. In 1798, Sir Alexander Crichton, M.D. wrote An *Inquiry Into the Nature and Origin of Mental Derangement*. Despite the title of his book, he was quite advanced in his approach to the topic. In his chapter on attention, he observed that some attention disorders are hereditary. Crichton described "a mental restlessness. In this disease of attention, if it can with propriety be called so, every impression seems to agitate the person, and gives him or her an unnatural degree of mental stress...They have a particular name for the state of their nerves, which is expressive enough of their feelings. They say they have the fidgets... These children need special education intervention...It is obvious that they had a severe problem in attending, even how hard they did try."

Contrast Dr. Crichton's approach with that of Dr. George Still, M.D. who is referred to as the father of British pediatrics. In March 1902, he presented a series of lectures on "some abnormal psychical conditions in children." He concluded that "there is a defect of moral consciousness which cannot be accounted for by any fault of the environment." When speaking of moral consciousness or moral control he meant, "the control of action in conformity with the idea of the good of all." Dr. Still described children who had serious problems with sustained attention and self-regulation, who were often aggressive, defiant, resistant to discipline and excessively emotional. He seemed to be describing children with oppositional defiant disorder. Of course, the concept of subtypes predated both Drs. Crichton and Still.

Dr. Samuel Orten (1879-1948) pioneered the study and treatment of learning disabilities. The Orton Gillingham method is based on his work with dyslexic children. It utilizes a multisensory, direct, explicit, sequential, structured, diagnostic and prescriptive approach to teaching. He was one of the first to describe the emotional aspects of dyslexia. According to his research, the majority of preschoolers were happy and well-adjusted. However, many studies have since been conducted on children and adults with dyslexia. Unfortunately, the findings often present far less positive outcomes.

Present-day studies of learning and attentional disorders investigate neurophysiological structures and functions along many variables. Areas tapped include age, gender, and comorbidity. Following is a small sample from each so my readers will learn the wide domains being explored, and may choose to pursue further knowledge in their fields of interest.

Current research (including technology, such as imaging devices) and clinical practices have found that many more areas of functioning than were originally theorized are impacted by learning and attentional disorders. Both deficits are thought to have genetic as well as environmental bases. It has now been determined that learning and attentional conditions often co-occur.

Initially, the terms Attention Deficit Disorder (ADD) and Attention Deficit and Hyperactivity Disorder (ADHA) were understood as related but different syndromes. However, now the term ADD is often subsumed under ADHD. When this syndrome was first identified, the focus was on children and adolescence. There was virtually no attention given to adults who had the characteristics of this syndrome. As male youngsters were relatively more likely to “act out” than females, it was assumed that this condition was almost exclusively gender-based. Currently, ADHD in female youngsters, as well as in adults of both sexes, is included in research and treatment. Very recently, practitioners are also reaching out to a previously underserved population: seniors with ADHD. While additional considerations must be given when prescribing medications to this age group, it is now understood that most can tolerate one or more of the increasing numbers of drugs developed for the symptoms of ADHD. There are a growing number of articles for the general public that offer coping skills for various age subpopulations. There is guidance for parents to deal with ADHD children. There are also articles to assist parents who have ADHD. Frequently, these adults have a child or children with the condition. In fact, I found that many parents who have ADHD children recognize the syndrome in themselves and seek treatment. ADDitude, an online magazine, is a wonderful source of information. It provides daily advice and instruction, much of which is free. As a mother who has learning/attentional challenges, I would have found this knowledge extremely helpful and reassuring when my son was young.

Dr. Russell Barkley is an internationally recognized authority on ADHD. He is credited with examining the relationship of executive functioning to self-regulation in individuals with ADHD. Barkley found that the preponderance of people with the most common form of ADHD have inordinate difficulty with sustaining attention; persevering toward goals; becoming distracted as they progress; being hyperactive; and inhibiting behaviors, words, ideas and feelings that may be socially inappropriate for the circumstances or incongruent with one's long-term objectives. ADHD is a disorder of self-regulation.

Dr. Ned Hallowell is a psychiatrist who has dedicated his professional life to the study of attentional disorders. He has redefined and renamed the syndrome. Through research and practice, he found that certain individuals with this disorder often have an abundance of attention and has coined the syndrome "variable attention stimulus trait." This model also recognizes that individuals with attentional disorders often are hypersensitive to criticism.

In a similar vein, Dr. William Dodson originally coined the term "rejection sensitivity dysphoria," to describe an extreme emotional sensitivity, guilt and shame to perceived rejection, suffered by those with attentional disorders. On the flip side, these individuals experience heightened energy and esteem with praise and approval.

Attentional disorders often coexist with many conditions, in addition to learning disabilities and rejection sensitive dysphoria. Complex ADHD is comorbidly associated with anxiety, tics, oppositional defiant disorder (ODD), mood disorders (including bipolar), and substance use disorder. This heterogeneity reflects the many factors that can affect how the syndrome is manifested. It is hypothesized that these conditions arise from a partly shared neuropsychological basis.

Dr. Daniel Amen has taken another approach to conceptualizing the heterogeneity of ADHD. He is one of many researchers and clinicians who has found that ADHD is composed of subtypes. Using non-invasive diagnostic tools, such as SPECT, he has studied blood flow and brain activity patterns of his patients. Amen found that there are seven different types of ADHD, each with its own symptoms and treatment choices. In his book, *Healing ADD: The Breakthrough Program That Allows You to See and Heal the Seven Types of ADD*, he explores three neurotransmitters: dopamine, serotonin, and GABA as well as the brain areas responsible for various functions. One area controls executive functions of concentration, attention span, judgment, organization, and planning. A second area helps the brain to shift gears and detect errors. A third area involves memory, learning, emotional reactions, mood stability and visual processing. Finally, there is a system in the brain that establishes emotional tone and bonding. I will summarize his subtypes and suggested treatments for each.

1. Classic ADD. Symptoms are inattention, distractibility, disorganization and impulsivity. Treatments: stimulant medications, such as Ritalin, Adderall, Vyvance or Concerta. Stimulant supplements, such as rhodiola, green tea, ginseng, the amino acid L-tyrosine and fish oil that is higher in EPA than in DHA are also recommended. Finally, physical activity beyond what has been exerted has been found to be beneficial.

2. Inattentive ADD. Symptoms are short attention span, distractibility, disorganization, procrastination, possible daydreaming and introversion. Treatments: stimulant medications and a high protein, lower carbohydrate diet.

3. Over-Focused ADD. Symptoms are the same as Classic ADD, in addition to trouble in shifting attention, going from thought to thought or task to task, getting stuck in negative thought patterns or behaviors. Treatments: supplements such as L-tryptophan, 5-HTP (dietary supplement used as an antidepressant); saffron, and inositol (naturally occurring nutrient used to boost alertness, focus, mood and mental clarity); otherwise antidepressants Effexor, Pristiq or Cymbalta; avoiding a high protein diet which may trigger negative behavior, neurofeedback.

4. Temporal Lobe ADD. Core symptoms of ADD, as well as learning, memory and behavior problems, such as quick anger, aggression and mild paranoia. Treatments: GABA to calm neural activity and inhibit nerve cells from over-firing or firing erratically; anticonvulsant medications to help with mood stability; gingko or vinpocetine to help with learning and memory problems.

5. Limbic ADD. Core symptoms of Classic ADD, as well as chronic low-level sadness (not depression): moodiness, low energy, frequent feelings of helplessness or excessive guilt and chronic low self-esteem. Treatments: supplements DL-phenylalanine (DLPA); L-tryosine, and SAMe (adenosyl-methionine); antidepressants Wellbutrin or Imipramine; exercise; fish oil and diet modifications.

6. Ring of Fire ADD. Symptoms are sensitivity to noise, light, touch; periods of mean, nasty behavior; unpredictable behavior; speaking quickly; anxiety and fearfulness. Treatments: stimulants alone may make the symptoms worse. Begin with an elimination diet. If allergy is expected, neurotransmitters GABA and serotonin are boosted through supplements; such as GABA, 5-HTP, L-tyrosine and medications if necessary. For medications, begin with anticonvulsants and the blood pressure drugs guanfacine and clonidine, which calm overall hyperactivity.

7. Anxious ADD. Core symptoms of Classis ADD, as well as anxiety and tension, having physical stress symptoms like headaches and stomachaches, predicting the worst, freezing in anxiety-provoking situations, especially if being judged. Treatments: Promote relaxation and increase dopamine and GABA levels. ADD stimulants, taken alone, make patients more anxious. Begin with a range of "calming" supplements, such asL-theanine, relora, magnesium, and holy basil. Tricyclic antidepressants Imipramine or Desipramine to lower anxiety, depending on the individual. Neurofeedback to decrease symptoms of anxiety.

One should never self-medicate or follow advice after reading any literature. Always discuss any proposed diet or addition of any substance with your doctor. Natural supplements can cause serious health conditions.

As I have written, ADHD may have negative consequences for academic achievement, as well as for employment performance and social relationships. However, it also may bring with it the advantage to think more creatively. In a March 5th, 2019 article for Neurological Health, Holly White has discussed three aspects of creative cognition found in many individuals with this disorder. They are divergent thinking, conceptual expansion and overcoming knowledge constraints. Divergent thinking is the capacity to think of many ideas from one starting point. Examples of this would be conceptualizing new uses for everyday objects or devising new features for innovative items. White notes that previous knowledge can be a barrier to creative thinking. Seeking to find inspiration from a model may result in what designers have referred to as "fixation." When individuals are shown a model from which to generate a novel example, they may incorporate features of that model, therefore limiting a fresh approach. Thus, the capacity to overcome this tendency is essential for creativity.

Conceptual expansion is the ability to loosen the boundaries of concepts. Semantic activation is a term to describe this capacity - the ability to "turn on" ideas that have been stored in memory. White cited her research which found that ADHD students demonstrated a greater degree of creative thinking than their neurotypical peers. She also noted that similar findings have been reported for gifted neurotypical students. White noted that while nonconformity may not seem extraordinary or important, a small modification may lead to a significant development. She concluded that ADHD often results in difficulty when performance demands sustained, focused attention. However, distractibility and a chaotic mindset can be an asset when creative thinking is required. An individual whose thinking is characterized by the above-described three aspects could be valuable in innovative fields.

Reaching a similar conclusion and applying it exigently, Taylor and Vestergaard (2022) stated, "Schools, academic institutions and workplaces are not designed to make the most of explorative thinking. But we urgently need to start nurturing this way of thinking to allow humanity to continue to adapt." Accommodations are one means of serving this purpose for individuals with "invisible disabilities." It is therefore of the utmost importance to be informed about what such an individual's needs are, as well as where and how these supports can be obtained.

Chapter 5

As is true of all college students, there is a great deal of information to consider in selecting a college. Its mission, location, size, courses and majors, tuition, financial aid and degree specifications, as well as services, should all be researched before reaching a decision. Students who have individualized learning requirements may have additional questions. In generating pertinent questions and evaluating responses received, students' solid understanding of their learning profiles may be very beneficial. What are the documentation requirements? Are evaluations offered, either gratis or for a fee? If not, are there referrals to local credentialed evaluators? What is the length of semesters? Can arrangements to receive and store medications be reasonably met ? Of course, issues pertaining to obtaining accommodations may be very important. The degree of assistance a student could benefit from may be a factor to consider. Landmark and Beacon, for instance, are wholly dedicated to students with special learning needs. It should be noted that, while providing accommodations is mandated for postsecondary students who are qualified and for whom barriers to learning exist, that is not true for services. However, there are a number of colleges, such as the University of Arizona, Texas Tech and Hofstra Universities that provide additional fee-based services for their LD/ADHD students. Finally, there are schools which include additional academic services in their tuition. Colleges also differ in the procedures required for accessing accommodations. What follows are examples of approaches, the information about which might be important for a student to have, in regard to his or her comfort level. A center for distraction-reduced testing may be used at one college, where it may be the instructor's responsibility to arrange for the testing site at another institution. It has been my experience that a prearranged location and specified procedure for testing tends to facilitate implementing the accommodation. Another procedural difference can be found in the manner in which instructors receive a student's accommodation instructions. In one school, the office that determines accommodations forwards that information to the professors. Alternatively, the student provides the information to the instructor, either directly or online.

I thought it would be useful to include a brief presentation of the process of obtaining accommodations. There is no age ceiling to granting accommodations. However, as is true of most interventions, the earlier they are administered, the better. Therefore, while my focus has been on the postsecondary student, I will describe the process when beginning in the K-12 setting. Ideally, a K-12 youngster identified as having significant learning challenges should be evaluated by the school psychologist to determine if the student meets the criteria for being accommodated, due to having a disability. Alternatively, parents may choose a qualified independent professional to administer an assessment if they prefer, or if the school refuses to do so. However, the cost can be prohibitive. Therefore, unfortunately, it is not unusual for parents to spend years obtaining a school-based evaluation, numerous attempts being made to convince them that their child is performing up to capacity.

This is less the case where the child's behaviors disrupt the class, such as the hyperactive student. Parents may make an appointment with their child's pediatrician or be referred by their youngster's doctor to a psychiatrist. An evaluation by a medical professional offers two benefits. First, the services may be covered by insurance, unlike most psychological assessments. A second benefit is that medication can be prescribed, which might produce behavioral changes more quickly than classroom adjustments. However, while those professionals are licensed to prescribe these drugs, they may not have the training required to diagnose and treat complex neurological conditions. Moreover, certain medications do improve symptoms, but have side effects which impair the very functions they are prescribed to alleviate. For example, certain medications given to improve concentration cause insomnia. The lack of sleep then impedes the ability to concentrate. Therefore, the side effects may preclude taking a drug. A prescriber may then adjust the dosage or try a different medication. Unfortunately, many of my college students experienced difficulties in their academic performance while transitioning from one medication to another. The fast pace of a semester often did not allow adequate time for their bodies to accommodate the drug-neither to get the benefit nor overcome the reaction. There was not always an academic allowance made for that. Many families do not have insurance that covers the prescribed drugs or the associated doctor visits. Finally, the medications can be addictive and studies have found an elevated incidence of substance abuse in the ADHD population. I always recommend that all accommodations be attempted before medications are given. If it is determined that medications would be beneficial, all reactions should be clearly explained, and administration monitored when indicated and possible.

There are a number of significant differences between the K-12 and post-secondary accommodation processes. As I previously wrote, the purpose of a K-12 accommodation is different from one granted at the college level. The objective of a K-12 accommodation is to promote success for the student. The function of an accommodation on the post-secondary level is equal access or the removal of a barrier to learning/performance. That being said, there continues to be confusion about the role of an IEP or 504 plan as documentation in securing postsecondary accommodations. Both could be helpful in providing information about a student's strengths and weaknesses, as well as what had been beneficial. However, there is no legal requirement for a college to offer the same accommodations that were provided in the K-12 setting. As I wrote earlier, all institutions of higher education that receive federal funds must, with few exceptions, provide the appropriate accommodations to students with documented disabilities. Unlike K-12, however, the legal definition of a qualified college or graduate student with a disability is relevant. It is one who must be able to meet the academic standards with or without an accommodation.

In a recent study, Weis and Bittner examined college students' access to academic support by accommodations, as a function of institutional type, selectivity, and cost over time. Although access to accommodations increased from 2.8% to 5.2% over the past 12 years, this change was largely driven by students attending the most selective and expensive private institutions. Access to accommodations was significantly lower and remained relatively stable among students attending two-year public colleges. The authors attribute this fact to the Matthew effect: students most in need of academic support are increasingly less likely to receive it. The authors suggest four ways to reduce this inequality:

(1) Encourage universal design (structures and instruction are accessible to all.)

(2) Facilitate access for students with disabilities from disadvantaged backgrounds.

(3) Critically evaluate documentation from students without real-world limitations.

(4) Insist on evidence of symptom or performance validity before granting accommodations.

No parent or young adult must disclose a disability to any school the student plans to attend or is attending. However, receiving an accommodation depends on presenting, in some form, the legitimate need for such to the proper certifying agent. Here too, there is a difference between the accommodation procedures in the K-12 and postsecondary settings. The college student is expected and encouraged to take the initiative by contacting the department responsible for providing disability services. In my experience, this is often difficult for the student or parent, at least at first. Most parents of students with "invisible disabilities" have had to advocate for their children throughout their schooling and are unaccustomed to letting their children handle this responsibility. I have worked with students who also were accustomed to having their parents take charge and were more comfortable with that arrangement. In contrast are the students who firmly did not intend to be accommodated and the parents who took over this role. Going forward, a student who is 18 years or older must give permission for a parent or anyone else to legally access his or her academic information.

It is important to understand the reasons why a student is reluctant to disclose a disability. There may be shame associated with the condition. The student may resist any form of labeling. He or she may assume that the painful, embarrassing, futile or even damaging procedures previously experienced will be repeated on the college level. While there is no guarantee that provisions will meet with expectations and be effective, there are advantages to receiving accommodations on the college level.

Yet another difference in accommodation procedures between K-12 and college is that professors are not given the student's documentation. As I previously wrote, they are, of course, given accommodation information by whatever practices the college has established.

As I previously wrote, it is considered standard practice for the student and a disability staff member to engage in the interactive process as a means of determining accommodations. This entails discussions that could cover academic history, areas of deficit and accommodations that were previously provided. In addition, observations of the student by a staff member may be illuminating. The disability professional's understanding of the manifestations of learning disorders in students, and the ability to develop rapport with the interviewee are essential to the process. When available, diagnostic evaluations are reviewed. They vary considerably in scope and detail. Unfortunately, they may also vary in quality and applicability to the academic environment.

Chapter 6

The psychoeducational evaluation generally taps global cognitive (learning) ability as well as achievement levels in academic content, such as reading (both the pronunciation of words and comprehension of material), mathematics, and written expression. A common approach to diagnosing a learning disability has been to determine whether the cognitive score is significantly higher than the achievement score(s). This finding suggests that the individual is currently underusing his/her intellectual potential in certain areas. Various measurement instruments of Intelligence Quotient (I.Q.) and achievement levels continue to proliferate.

The most comprehensive testing is a neuropsychological evaluation. This is generally administered if the student has suffered a traumatic brain injury or has/had a neurological disorder or disease significantly affecting cognitive functioning. Examples would be a stroke, meningitis, or multiple sclerosis. This assessment often consists of a psychoeducational evaluation and provides additional information about the relationship between brain functioning and deficit performance. As is true of psychoeducational evaluations, the number of testing batteries continues to grow.

Some schools will specify that certain testing instruments be used. The age of documentation may also be a factor. Previously, many colleges would not consider documentation older than three years. Currently, most schools are more flexible with this criterion. Should documentation be insufficient or unavailable, many schools will give a student accommodations on a temporary or provisional basis, until acceptable documentation is offered. This may also be true for conditions that are temporary. Provisional accommodations are important as they allow for time to arrange for testing and/or the financial resources to cover the costs. Some flexibility on the part of a college may determine whether a student can attend there, as retesting may be prohibitively expensive.

I have addressed issues pertaining to postsecondary requirements for documentation. Evaluations frequently play an important role in determining accommodations. While the information that they provide may be very useful, I believe it is important to view the findings in context. Unfortunately, however, the general public has very little information about the many variables that should be taken into account in understanding test results. Some are inherent in the construction of the test. For example, what is not covered, how well items capture content, and directions to the administrator should be considered. Other variables lie in the physical environment of the testing room. The student's performance could be impacted by distracting sights and sounds as well as the room's temperature. The individual's test taking attitudes as well as current state of health and stresses external to the test should also be taken into account.

The testee's educational experiences are extremely important. I have worked with students who were initially diagnosed with significant deficits attributed to learning disorder(s), but in other areas of functioning were gifted. Lack of exposure to material they couldn't access when accommodations were not given lowered their scores. Furthermore, these students often were removed from classes for special help, therefore missing additional material. Even worse, many students reported to me that the assistance was of limited value. Paradoxically and tragically, the re-evaluation before graduation indicated the student was now classified as Below Average. Therefore, while a test has been found to provide useful information, it should not be viewed as a static, comprehensive description of an individual's intellectual capabilities. Unfortunately, it often is.

Over the course of my training, I learned that a highly skilled and experienced psychologist plays a vitally important role in determining the value of the report derived from testing. The examiner's ability to develop rapport with the student, and his/her interpretive capacities, are critically important. Furthermore, the capacity to supersede some of the test limitations by "testing the limits" greatly broadens and deepens the reader's understanding of the student. This procedure goes beyond scoring an individual's failure to respond to an item or incorrectly answer an item. It is very useful to know why an individual did not do well and if some modification would improve the score. One approach, on a timed test, would be for the examiner to return to the unfinished or incorrect item(s) and see if allowing additional time or any appropriate modification improves the score. The original score remains unchanged, but this added information is very helpful in determining accommodations.

Here is an example of the importance of the tester's understanding and inclusion in the report of why a student did not do well on a particular portion(s) of a test. As a student, I observed a psychologist about to test a young adult. I noticed that one of the subject's hands was in a cast. (I learned that it was his right and dominant hand.) He was given a timed task that purported to tap a number of capabilities. The psychologist's subsequent report made no mention of the fact that the subject had very limited use of his dominant hand. Interpretations of his poor performance assumed deficits in several areas that were based on the assumption that he had use of both hands. The conclusions were not valid and may have had very significant impacts on the young man's future life. My experience of this clearly made a profound and long-lasting impression on me. This, and other similar and powerful lessons, are why I dedicated my life and this book to the populations I have served.

Unfortunately, today, many individuals continue to remain undiagnosed or misdiagnosed. Others have not been treated or have been inappropriately treated. Student after student disclosed to me substance abuse in their attempts to self-medicate or deal with the stresses and painful ramifications of their conditions. Not a few contemplated suicide. Finally, it was also not a rare occurrence for students to reveal that they had been institutionalized or incarcerated.

Chapter 7

Despite the consequences of failures in clinical and educational settings, there are promising advances. The proliferation of assistive technology is a very important paradigm shift. Currently, many academic tasks that represent barriers for students can be overcome through technology. I will offer some specific information regarding resources to access technology in the next section. For now, know that printed material can be converted to sound and oral material can be converted to text. A number of technical services can automate note-taking, supplementing or replacing peer notes. There are calculators designed to compensate for various deficits. Unfortunately, however, there is limited availability of technology in grades K-12 for several reasons. One issue is funding shortages. Another is resistance from administrators and instructors, who believe that, for instance, "It's not reading if you hear rather than see material." Recordings may be legitimate for blind students but not always for those with dyslexia and ADHD. It has been my experience that there is considerably less resistance to the use of assistive technology in institutions of higher education than in grades K-12. With a few exceptions, remediation of the basic skills is not available on the college level. As professors do not see their role as providing instruction in those areas, compensation by the use of assistive technology is more acceptable.

Yet another paradigm shift is the move from accommodating individual students to making environments welcoming to all people. This literally groundbreaking concept which underlies both architecture as well as classroom policies and procedures is called Universal Design (UD.) The objective of UD is to ensure that structures and instruction are accessible to all. In fact, adhering to the principles of UD has proven advantageous to those who are not disabled as well as to those who are. In their article in The Journal of Postsecondary Education and Disability, David Leake and Robert Stodden described the importance of UD. "Leading theories of persistence in higher education highlight both academic integration and social integration, as reflected in having a sense of 'belonging' on campus, as key factors for student success. Emerging trends suggest that the next phase of progress for students with disabilities in higher education will be establishing and implementing shared norms about what it takes to make a campus barrier free and welcoming-a place where disability is not seen as a marker of membership in a 'special group' virtually nobody wants to be a part of but is, rather, accepted and appreciated as an element in a valued range of diversity."

While most colleges generally offer tutoring, there is a greatly expanded and much more detailed description of strategies both by universities and by individual practitioners. A professional whose work I admire is Elizabeth Hamblet, whose website is https://ldadvisory. She is a learning consultant and has written two books - *From High School to College: Steps to Success for Students With Disabilities and Transitioning to College: A Guide for Students With Disabilities.* Elizabeth also has an online magazine, a blog and a podcast. I will just list the areas she provides information on for college students with special needs. As with other material designed for a particular population, many of these strategies would benefit all students.

- Time Management
- Study Strategies
- Reading Assignments
- SQ3R
- Difficult Courses
- Online Organization
- Long Term Assignments
- Course Substitutions
- Registering for Accommodations

The last paradigm shift under discussion is the growth of coaching services. While focused on students with learning/attentional disorders, it has been found to be beneficial for any student. Coaching professionals state that the service they provide differs from counseling and from tutoring. There are a growing number of organizations who credential those who participate in their training. In an AHEAD Webinar, Drs. David R. Parker and Sharon Field provided the following information about the goals and techniques of coaching. In brief, self- determination, which incorporates autonomy, relatedness and competence, is a primary goal. They elaborated, stating that self-determination, resilience and grit, incorporating passion and persistence, are essential for success. Coaches empower their students through encouraging their use of positive self-talk, enhanced follow-through, and wider use of available resources.

Chapter 8

The final section of my book is dedicated to the tremendous growth of resources for individuals with disabilities in all stages and circumstances of life. The following list is not exhaustive. However, one contact will lead to others, so hopefully, readers will find the information and assistance they are seeking.

Information on Assistive Equipment/Accessible Technology/Accommodations:
dusek@augsburg.edu

- Reading
- Writing
- Note Taking
- Dictation-Speech to Text and Speech Recognition
- Mind Mapping and Brainstorming
- Study Skills and Aids
- Organization and Task Management
- Time Management
- Distraction Free/Reduced Environment
- Research Tools
- Stress Management and Relaxation
- Vision Support
- Auditory Support
- Communication Support
- Built In Accessibility

Associations and Organizations

ADA Centers-Regional Technical Centers for the American online directory of every law related to disability
adata.org

AHEAD-Association on Higher Education and Disability
www.ahead.org

The National Center for College Students with Disabilities Clearinghouse and Resource Library
https://www.nccsdclearinghouse.org

DREAM-Disability Rights, Education, Activism and Mentoring Student group providing online resources and community for all students with disabilities across the country. Offering a weekly email newsletter and national conference.

CHADD-National Resource on ADHD
chadd.org

Delta Alpha Phi. This is the Honor Society for post-secondary students with disabilities
deltaalphapihonorsociety.org

DO-IT Disabilities, Opportunities, Internet and Technology. Free Publications and Videos for Disabled Students
Washington.edu/doit/what-qualified-student-disability

LD advisory.com
https://www.ldadvisory.com/collegestudents

LDonline

Centralized site for all resources related to learning disabilities and ADHD. Has resources for college students

LDOnline.org

National Center for Learning Disabilities (NCLD)

www.ncld.org

National Joint Committee on Learning Disabilities

njcld.org

National Technical Assistance Center on Transition

transitionta.org

Pacer Center

Provides information for parents on various aspects of disability including transition to higher education

www.pacer.org

Guides

- K&W Guide to Colleges for Students with Learning Differences
- Peterson's Guide to Colleges
- The Princeton Review

Scholarships

JFK Profile In Courage Scholarship

https://www.jfklibrary.org/learn/education/profile-in-courage-essay-contest/getting-started-First

Award is $10,000

Lime Connect Scholarships
https://www.limeconnect.com/programs/page/scholarships-merit
For current students
Microsoft disAbility renewable scholarships
$5,000 a year

scholarships@seattlefoundation.org
Targeting high school students who intend to pursue a career in technology

Nitro College
https://www.nitrocollege.com/scholarships/disabilities

Commercial sites may contact you to collect information and add you to their mailing lists.

References

Amen, D.G. Healing ADD: The Breakthrough Program That Allows You to See and Heal the 7 types of ADD. 464 pgs. Berkley Books. 2013.

Areej, A. Perceptions of Using Assistive Technology For Students With Disabilities in the Classroom. International Journal of Special Education. v.3, n.1, 2018.

Barkley, R.A. Executive Functions-What They Are, How They Work and Why They Evolved. 244 pgs, Guilford Publications, May 2012.

Crichton, A. An Inquiry Into The Nature and Origin

of Mental Derangement: Comprehending a Concise System Of the Human Mind and History of the Passions and Their Effects. Volume 1, 1798.

Dodson, W. Rejection Sensitive Dysphoria: Symptom Test for ADHD Brains. ADDiTUDE, February 28, 2022.

French, M. The Women's Room. Summit Books, Jan 1, 1977. 471 pages.

Friedan, B. The Feminine Mystique. W.W. Norton, Feb 11, 1963. 593 pages.

Hallowell, E. & Ratey, J. ADHD 2.0: New Science and Essential Strategies For Thriving With Distraction-From Childhood Through Adulthood. 208 pgs. Ballantine Books, 2021.

Hamblet, E. From High School to College: Steps to Success for Students With Disabilities. Council for Exceptional Children, 2017.

Leake, D. & Stodden, R. Journal of Postsecondary and Disability v.27, n.4. pgs 399-408. Win 2014.

Orten, S. Reading, Writing and Speech Problems in Children and Selected Papers.(The PRO-ED classics series)by Samuel Torrey Orton. 1988-11-06.

Parker, D.R. & Field, S. Grit, Self-Determination and Coaching. AHEAD Webinar, October 13, 2020.

Raue, K. and Lewis, L. (2011.) Students with Disabilities at Degree-Granting Postsecondary Institutions (NCES 2011-2018). U.S. Department of Education, National Center for Education Statistics. Washington, D.C: U.S. Government Printing Office.

Simpson, E. Reversals: A Personal Account of Victory over Dyslexia.HoughtonMifflin,1979. 246 pages.

Still, G. Common Disorders and Diseases of Childhood. Paperback. London: Hodder and Stoughton, August 25, 2016. 832 pgs.

Taylor, H. & Vestergaard, M.D.(2022). Developmental Dyslexia: Disorder or Specialization in Exploration? Frontiers in Psychology,>https://doi.org/10.3389/fpsyg.2022.889245.

U.S. Department of Education. National Center for Education Statistics. 2021.Digest Of Educational Statistics 2019 (2021-2022.)

Weis, R., Bittner, S.A. College Students' Access to Academic Accommodations Over Time: Evidence of a Matthew Effect In Higher Education Psychol.Inj. and Law 15, 236-252 (2022.)

White, H. The Creativity of ADHD. Scientific American, March 5, 2019.

Acknowledgements

Many people had a hand in bringing this book to publication. First of all, I would like to thank my family: my husband, Nicholas Kushner; my son, Erik Koestenblatt; and my parents, Sally and Al Charney. I also want to express my gratitude to Auctus publisher Dr. Shrikrishna Singh, graphic designer Colleen Cummings, and my editor, Scott Spires. In the interest of privacy, I have changed the names of some of the people who appear in this book.

About the author

Marlene K. Kushner, Ed.D., a native of Brooklyn, New York, Marlene traveled westward as she completed her education to become a psychologist. She earned a B.A., cum laude, at Hunter College of the City University of New York, and was inducted into Psi Chi, The National Honor Society of Psychology. Following that, she was awarded a M.A. in Clinical Psychology from Fairleigh Dickinson University. Marlene became a New Jersey Certified School Psychologist through a program at Montclair State University and then earned a national certification. During this time, she learned, quite incidentally, that she herself had a number of learning disabilities. She concluded her formal studies at Indiana University of Pennsylvania, receiving an Ed.D, with a specialization in The Neuropsychology of Learning Disorders.

Throughout her studies and career, Marlene has sought to advance the knowledge about and opportunities for individuals who learn differently. She has served as an accommodation specialist in disability centers at a number of colleges and universities. In addition to working with students, she has given presentations to faculties and authored papers for professionals as well as for the general public.

Marlene was a pioneer in the emerging field of post-secondary disability service. She was appointed to The Advisory Board of the New Jersey Department of Higher Education. Its mission was to establish guidelines for programs serving college students with learning disabilities. She also has been a longstanding member of The Association on Higher Education and Disability. Marlene was awarded Ushkow Foundation grants to evaluate cognitive remediation programs and programs for learning disabled college students. The Association for Children and Adults with Learning Disabilities has honored her with a Certificate of Recognition.

Printed in the USA
CPSIA information can be obtained
at www.ICGtesting.com
CBHW070351201223
2691CB00005BA/21